CITYSPOTS
DUBLIN

Pat Levy

Written by Pat Levy
Front cover photography courtesy of Doug McKinlay/Lonely Planet Images
Series design based on an original concept by Studio 183 Limited

Produced by Cambridge Publishing Management Limited
Project editor: Catherine Burch
Layout: Trevor Double
Maps: PC Graphics
Republic of Ireland maps: reproduced from Ordnance Survey Ireland Permit No. 8226
© Ordnance Survey Ireland and Government of Ireland
Transport map: © Communicarta Limited

Published by Thomas Cook Publishing
A division of Thomas Cook Tour Operations Limited
Company Registration No. 1450464 England
PO Box 227, Unit 18, Coningsby Road
Peterborough PE3 8SB, United Kingdom
email: books@thomascook.com
www.thomascookpublishing.com
+ 44 (0) 1733 416477

ISBN-13: 978-184157-623-7
ISBN-10: 1-84157-623-9

First edition © 2006 Thomas Cook Publishing
Text © 2006 Thomas Cook Publishing
Maps © 2006 Thomas Cook Publishing
Series Editor/Project Editor: Kelly Anne Pipes
Production/DTP: Steven Collins

Printed and bound in Spain by GraphyCems

All rights reserved. No part of this publication may be reproduced, stored in a retrieval system or transmitted, in any form or by any means, electronic, mechanical, recording or otherwise, in any part of the world, without prior permission of the publisher. Requests for permission should be made to the publisher at the above address.

Although every care has been taken in compiling this publication, and the contents are believed to be correct at the time of printing, Thomas Cook Tour Operations Limited cannot accept any responsibility for errors or omission, however caused, or for changes in details given in the guidebook, or for the consequences of any reliance on the information provided. Descriptions and assessments are based on the author's views and experiences when writing and do not necessarily represent those of Thomas Cook Tour Operations Limited.

CONTENTS

INTRODUCING DUBLIN
Introduction.....................6
When to go.....................8
Bloomsday......................12
History............................14
Lifestyle..........................16
Culture............................18

MAKING THE MOST OF DUBLIN
Shopping........................22
Eating & drinking........24
Entertainment & nightlife.....28
Sport & relaxation.......32
Accommodation..........34
The best of Dublin......40
Something for nothing...........44
When it rains................46
On arrival......................48

THE CITY OF DUBLIN
Grafton Street &
  surrounding area........60
Temple Bar &
  surrounding area.......74
O'Connell Street &
  surrounding area.......86
West of the city centre.........100

OUT OF TOWN
The northern coastline &
  Newgrange..................116
South of the city..........130

PRACTICAL INFORMATION
Directory.......................144
Emergencies................156

INDEX............................158

MAP LIST
Dublin city......................50
Dublin transport...........55
Grafton Street &
  surrounding area........61
Temple Bar &
  surrounding area........75
O'Connell Street &
  surrounding area........87
West of the city centre.........101
Northern coastline &
  Newgrange..................117
South of the city..........131

CITYSPOTS

SYMBOLS & ABBREVIATIONS
The following symbols are used throughout this book:

ⓐ address   ⓣ telephone   ⓕ fax   ⓔ email   ⓦ website address
ⓞ opening times   ⓟ public transport connections   ⓘ important

The following symbols are used on the maps:

- information office
- airport
- hospital
- police station
- bus station
- railway station
- metro
- cathedral
- ❶ numbers denote featured cafés & restaurants

- ○ city
- ○ large town
- ○ small town
- = motorway
- — main road
- — minor road
- — railway

Hotels and restaurants are graded by approximate price as follows:
£ budget   **££** mid-range   **£££** expensive

▶ *Take a walk over the famous Ha'penny Bridge*

INTRODUCING Dublin

INTRODUCING DUBLIN

Introduction

Dublin is a curious mix of ancient and modern. On the one hand the city celebrates its Viking past and on the other erects gorgeous low-rise, ecologically sound, high-tech buildings on vast tracts of old warehouses that have lain derelict for generations. It rejoices in its membership of the EU and its role in peace-keeping but remembers the 200 or so martyrs of the doomed-to-fail 1916 Uprising; it consults with its nearest neighbour, Britain, on matters of importance but go into any pub when there's a football match between England and any other country in the world, and see whose side Dubliners are on.

Dublin is a great place to visit. It has its tourist infrastructure so polished you can see your face in it, hotels are online, wireless, hip places, or, if you prefer, quaint, 'olde worlde', loaded with antiques and full of ethnic charm. People come here for the *craic* (Irish fun); Dubliners really know how to enjoy themselves, and they exercise that talent at every opportunity. Dublin's bars and clubs heave with punters at weekends, big names perform at the Point and other venues, there are festivals coming out of the woodwork, culture in the form of classic theatre and opera, classical music hits you at every turn and there are more museums than you can shake a guidebook at. If all that sounds exhausting, the countryside is a 30-minute ride away on the DART rail system. Spend a day in the Wicklow hills or stride the bracing cliff walk at Howth.

And food! No longer the gravy dinner, meat and two veg capital of the world, Dublin can offer you every cuisine imaginable, nipped and tucked to suit both the Irish palate and the diversity of the wallet content of its visitors. And the glory of the city is its size; tiny by the standards of any British city, all the places you really want to

INTRODUCTION

see are within walking distance of your hotel. Besides a guarantee of perfect weather (which they're working on, if they haven't sorted it out yet), can you ask for anything more?

🔺 *Government buildings - a prominent work of Edwardian architecture*

INTRODUCING DUBLIN

When to go

SEASONS & CLIMATE
Weather-wise there's no telling when is the perfect time to visit Dublin. Its weather is notoriously changeable and you are just as likely to get two weeks of drizzle in the middle of August as blazing sunshine and bright sunny January days rather than grey, overcast ones. But, generally speaking, temperatures are quite mild all year, with very few days below zero even in February. Summer temperatures average between 15 and 20°C (59 and 68°F), although the occasional scorcher of 26°C (79°F) or more has been known, while winter temperatures range between 5 and 10°C (41 and 50°F), with the odd few days of traffic chaos, flight delays and crunchy pavements while they remember where they left the gritting lorries. If you are intent on partying, the weather really doesn't affect you; the clubs and pubs open regardless of the weather, although if you are a smoker you might want to consider that you'll be standing shivering in a 'beer garden' while you get your fix. In summer the city is at its best – blossom on the trees, the parks looking like those pictures they use for jigsaw puzzles, the boat rides working, museums all open and lots and lots of open-air events.

ANNUAL EVENTS
Lots of the events listed here change their dates from year to year. Check the listed websites for the current year's dates and visit www.festivals.ireland.ie for a more comprehensive list.

January
Temple Bar Festival of Irish Culture (26–29 Jan).
ⓦ www.templebartrad.com

WHEN TO GO

February
Rugby Six Nations Championship matches (several weekends in Feb and Mar), the Irish home games of the annual rugby championships between Ireland, England, France, Italy, Scotland and Wales. Very big events in the city. ⓦ www.irishrugby.ie
Jameson Dublin International Film Festival (10 days in mid-Feb).
ⓦ www.dubliniff.com

March
St Patrick's Day celebrations (15–19 Mar), including a parade, green beer, lots of music in the pubs, late opening bars.
ⓦ www.stpatricksfestival.ie

▲ *Sean Tyrell at the Temple Bar Festival of Irish Culture*

INTRODUCING DUBLIN

April
Handel's Messiah (one day in mid-Apr), to celebrate the original performance of the Messiah which took place in Dublin. Performed (usually) in Neal's Music Hall. 01 677 2255

May
International Gay Dublin Theatre Festival (first week in May).
www.dublingaytheatrefestival.com

June
Diversions (June–Sept), a summer-long series of events based in the city, and especially in Temple Bar, ranging from free talks, musical performances and exhibitions to activities in the parks for children.
Flora Women's Mini Marathon (first weekend in June).
www.womensminimarathon.ie
Dublin Writer's Festival (mid-June).
www.dublinwritersfestival.com
Bloomsday (16 June, see page 12). www.jamesjoyce.ie

August
Dublin Gay and Lesbian Film Festival (first weekend in Aug).
www.gnc.ie/dlgff.ie
Dun Laoghaire Festival of World Cultures (last weekend in Aug).
www.festivalofworldcultures.com
The Liffey Swim (late Aug/early Sept), in which 400 or more contestants swim 2½ km (1½ miles) from Rory O'More Bridge to Custom House Quay. A weird sight.

September
GAA All-Ireland Senior Hurling Final (early Sept). www.gaa.ie

WHEN TO GO

Baileys Irish Championship Stakes (9 Sept or thereabouts).
ⓦ www.leopardstown.com
Dublin Fringe Theatre Festival. ⓦ www.fringefest.ie

October
Dublin Theatre Festival (first two weeks of Oct).
ⓦ www.theatrefestival.com
Dublin City Marathon (late Oct). ⓦ www.adidasdublincitymarathon.ie

December
Leopardstown Christmas Racing Festival (26–29 Dec).
ⓦ www.leopardstown.com

> **PUBLIC HOLIDAYS**
> On public holidays lots of shops close or have shorter hours, banks close and sights either close or operate with Sunday opening hours. Check each sight before you visit. Pubs close altogether on Good Friday (not a public holiday) and Christmas Day.
>
> **New Year's Day** 1 January
> **St Patrick's Day** 17 March
> **Easter Monday** Monday following Easter Day
> **May Holiday** First Monday in May
> **June holiday** First Monday in June
> **August Holiday** First Monday in August
> **August Holiday** Last Monday in August
> **Christmas Day** 25 December
> **St Stephen's Day** 26 December

INTRODUCING DUBLIN

Bloomsday

Bloomsday celebrates one of the most important, and probably least read, novels of the 20th century. In *Ulysses*, James Joyce writes about the peregrinations of an advertising salesman around the city of Dublin on 16 June 1904. He is the Jew, Leopold Bloom, an outsider and wanderer like Ulysses, and each of the chapters of the novel corresponds to an event from Homer's *Odyssey*. As he wrote the book, Joyce (living in exile in Europe – 'Ireland is the old sow that eats her farrow', his alter ego Stephen Dedalus says) carefully reconstructed the streets and buildings of the city, writing home to family and friends to check that Bloom's footsteps were perfect. Over the last decade or so, the small numbers of intellectuals celebrating the novel informally on 16 June has swelled to hundreds. The day now involves, besides the talks and tours and guest speakers, hundreds of people dressed up in Edwardian costumes, at each of the major sites of events in the novel and at the times that Bloom was fictionally there. If you have never read the novel, no matter – very few people taking part have. The people at each sight will tell you the story and you can join one of the groups following sections of Bloom's walk (the entire novel would be exhausting). The chemist shop, Swenys, sells out of lemon-scented soap (Bloom buys the soap there for his bath in the public bath house), Davy Byrne's, 'the moral pub', sells tonnes of gorgonzola cheese and burgundy (Bloom's lunch) and Stephen Dedalus lives again in the Martello Tower in Sandycove. Check the website (www.jamesjoyce.ie) to see which sites are being focused on the year you visit, but look out for events at Eccles Street (Bloom's home), Brown Thomas in Grafton Street, Davy Byrne's in Duke Street, College Green, St Andrew's Church in

BLOOMSDAY

Westland Row, Temple Bar, the Ormond Hotel and the Martello Tower in Sandycove.

The irony of it all is that *Ulysses* was banned in Ireland for decades, long after other countries had recognised its value as literature. Better late than never.

⬤ *James Joyce: one of the most famous writers of the 20th century*

INTRODUCING DUBLIN

History

Things went well in Ireland for a long time; the Stone Age, St Patrick, Christianity… all progress of a kind. During Europe's Dark Ages, the 6th, 7th and 8th centuries, Ireland was a beacon of humanity and learning, with its own laws, customs and schools, and Dublin was a settlement among many others with a mixture of Vikings and Gaels living in relative harmony. Dublin got bigger, minted its own coins and built a thingmote for public discussion at what is now College Green. In the 12th century, the English turned up, killed a bunch of people, bullied their way into the city, and then, like the Vikings before them, succumbed to the persuasive charms of the Irish, intermarried, took up speaking Gaelic, and all was well – for a time.

In 1536 Henry VIII needed some extra cash and wanted a new wife so he disestablished the Church of England, closed all the Irish monasteries and started the real trouble. In 1607 many of the leading noblemen fled from Ireland, unwilling to take up the new religion and rule. Dublin became a military town, its Catholic majority ruled by a few heavily armed Protestants. Dublin prospered, grew, had beautiful buildings built under British rule, but no one was very happy about it. In 1690 James II attempted to take Ireland back from the Protestant William of Orange and his defeat led to the penal laws against Catholics. The Catholic Irish majority of the city were denied the right to own land, practise their religion and, later, vote.

The centuries since that time are marked in Dublin's history as a series of failed rebellions against the British. In 1798 the United Irishmen were based in the city and were defeated by government troops. In 1803 a spectacularly unsuccessful coup took place in Dublin led by Robert Emmet. In 1829 things improved slightly when

Daniel O'Connell, a Catholic, was voted into the British Parliament and the last of the penal laws against Catholics was repealed. In 1845–49 Dublin was filled with thousands of desperate, starving people searching for food as the potato crop repeatedly failed for four years. 1867 saw further loss of life as the Irish Republican Brotherhood tried their hand at getting rid of the British. In 1870 land reform allowed Irish tenant farmers to buy their land, but not their freedom from British rule. Then in 1916 about 2,000 dedicated, idealistic men and women tried to take the city, stir the population to arms and send the British packing. It didn't work. The leaders were executed and people have been dying with photographs of the martyrs in their pockets ever since.

The year 1921 saw the signing of the Anglo-Irish Treaty and the resulting, less-than-successful independence of southern Ireland. The Irish took to fighting each other for a couple of years and then settled down to banning everything from contraception to *Ulysses*. Seventy years or so of economic depression, emigration and travelling to Britain for abortions and condoms followed, and then the Celtic Tiger was born, transforming the Irish economy. Sadly, the political repercussions of Henry VIII are still with us.

INTRODUCING DUBLIN

Lifestyle

Dublin is a modern, forward-looking, European city, its workforce one of the youngest and most well-educated in Europe. With a huge student population and thousands of young Eastern Europeans willing to take up unskilled work, it is no wonder that there is so much for young people to do, and so many opportunities to spend hard-earned money in the city. The city's weekends are for the young; after midnight the central streets belong to the party-goers and it is possible to spend the entire weekend without sobering up if only you know the right places to go. Dublin's young don't remember when condoms were a political issue or a green card was a means of getting some prospects. Some form unions not sanctioned by the Church, become single parents, adopt lifestyles that their parents never dreamed of, own their own flats in regenerated parts of the city, plan to buy a second home in the Irish countryside, and go to church only for weddings and funerals and special occasions or perhaps don't go at all.

Dublin is a family city too. Outside the city centre with its clubs and shops, life in the suburbs is a quieter, slower business. Many families still observe the old ways of life – three or more children, church on Sundays, or even daily, family dinners in the evening while watching *Coronation Street* or one of the Sky channels, the extended family close by. They sigh over the many tribunals investigating all sorts of corruption, tut over the number of foreigners in their city (although many of them would come to the defence of anyone being abused) and plan their holidays somewhere warm away from the Dublin weather.

Lots of Dubliners are newcomers, people who have moved to the city from small Irish towns or from further afield, Europe, the

LIFESTYLE

US or Africa. For the first time, Dublin has a sizeable population of non-Christians of all kinds, lapsed or otherwise; more people speak Chinese in the city than Gaelic; and all shades of colour can be seen making a life in what was for centuries a Christian, conservative monoculture.

▲ *The irresistible St Patrick's Day festivities*

INTRODUCING DUBLIN

Culture

Even if the most popular form of culture in Dublin is found at the bottom of a pint glass, there are other forms of culture alive and kicking in the city. Dublin has a strong, if conservative, theatre tradition, a huge live music repertoire from classical and operatic to traditional bands, jazz and rock, a strong dance tradition covering classical ballet, Riverdance clones and modern dance and salsa classes. Its art galleries are remarkable for such a small country and its museums are lively hands-on places, often providing the venue for free performances and recitals. Most of all, the streets and parks themselves are like galleries, with some stunning (and occasionally naff) street art to which Dubliners have affectionately given nicknames.

Theatre buffs will enjoy Dublin's offerings. The theatre festival in September, accompanied by a fringe festival, brings in theatre groups from around the world and every venue is booked for middle-of-the-road drama, experimental drama, and everything in between. The Gate, the Abbey, Andrew's Lane Studio, The Crypt, the Gaiety, Project, and of course the Helix, all have material on offer during the festival. But even outside festival time it is worth checking the listings magazines (see page 20) for theatrical happenings. 2006 saw excellent performances of many of Beckett's plays and there is always something to watch.

Classical music and opera is less obvious in the city but it thrives quietly. Here again, the listings are essential. The city has two orchestras, the National Symphony Orchestra and the RTÉ Concert Orchestra, both using the National Concert Hall as their main venue but performing in other places too. Opera Ireland puts on a season of works every other year at the Gaiety and there are regular

CULTURE

chamber music concerts at Project, The Crypt, Christchurch Cathedral, Dublin City Gallery, and St Stephen's Church (🅰 Mount St Upper ☎ 01 288 0663).

Two modern dance troupes operate out of Dublin: the Irish Modern Dance Theatre and the Dance Theatre of Ireland. For

🔺 *Taking Irish music to the streets*

INTRODUCING DUBLIN

> **STREET ART**
> Many of the city's pieces of street art have been given nicknames by Dubliners; 'the queer with the sneer' for the statue of Oscar Wilde in Merrion Square, 'the tart with the cart' for the Molly Malone statue, 'the hags with the bags' for a statue of two women chatting, 'the stiletto in the ghetto' for the tower of light, to name a few. In 1999 an enormous clock on a pole, counting down to the millennium, was inserted into the Liffey River. It became known as 'the time in the slime'. When it broke down and was removed, its name changed overnight to 'the gap in the crap'.

performances by them and other visiting dance ensembles, consult the listings.

Many of the city's museums and galleries were purpose-built and begun in the 19th century. The National Museum has an enormous collection of historical artefacts; much of its collection of decorative arts has moved to the old Collins Barracks. Art galleries have benefited from several donations to the state, including the collection from Russborough House, Hugh Lane's collection of art, and the art collection of Chester Beatty.

Listings for most cultural events and performances are to be found in the magazines *Event Guide* (also available online at www.eventguide.ie) and *In Dublin* (also available online at www.indublin.ie), which can be picked up for free from cafés, newsagents and hotels.

▶ *Beautiful but imposing government buildings*

✓ MAKING THE MOST OF Dublin

MAKING THE MOST OF DUBLIN

Shopping

It's not the place you'd take a plane to in order to do your shopping, but Dublin has some good offerings for the consumer. The city has two major shopping areas; Grafton Street, where the Irish Institution, Brown Thomas and lots of British chain stores line the pedestrianised street, topped by the busy St Stephen's Green Shopping Centre, and O'Connell Street and its side roads where there are several British and Irish department stores, numerous malls, a street market and lots of odd discount stores, especially along Earl Street North and Talbot Street.

Prices in the shops in Dublin fluctuate against prices in UK shopping centres. The chain stores often put the price in both sterling and euros on their goods, so you can see what you would be paying in England for the same item. The number of people in border towns such as Dundalk who make shopping trips over the border into the north to do their shopping rather suggests, though, that there are better bargains to be had in Northern Ireland.

The things to look out for in Dublin are the many attractive, hand-made clothes and housewares, made in small workshops all over the country and for sale in shops such as the Kilkenny Store (see page 68) or other shops along Nassau Street, Leinster Street South and Dawson Street. Look out for hand-made and hand-woven tweed outfits, hand-knitted jumpers, beautiful, imaginative jewellery crafted in silver and other metals, pottery ranging from things to hold spent matchsticks to entire dinner services with matching cloths and lamps. Ironwork, too, has moved on from curly magazine holders to some beautiful minimalist lamps, tables, or sets of glass and wrought-iron drinking glasses.

SHOPPING

Of course if it's something for the in-laws you're after, Dublin has that too – in bucket-loads. Felt leprechauns, tea towels with funny doggerel poems, giant green, gold and white hats with false hair sticking out, sets of Irish coffee glasses with the instructions printed on the side, shillelaghs... it's all still here.

● *Would you trust them to guard your treasures?*

MAKING THE MOST OF DUBLIN

Eating & drinking

Dublin is awash with restaurants of all qualities from fast food to foodie heaven and, with the city's high rents and the enormous competition, many of them, like Janis Joplin, live fast and die young. This year's place to be seen munching turns into next year's place to avoid at all costs and the next thing you know it's a mobile phone shop. You're best to look out for the places that offer traditional Irish

● *Eat and drink at a pavement café*

EATING & DRINKING

cooking with a modern twist, where you'll be able to try dishes such as champ (mashed potatoes and scallions mixed with lots of butter), boxty (potato and flour pancakes), colcannon (cabbage and potato), or some of the traditional Irish breads such as soda farls, leavened with bicarbonate of soda instead of yeast. Ethnic cuisines also feature largely in what was once a meat and two veg city. There are excellent Mexican, Italian, Indian and Thai places all serving innovative dishes, even an inexpensive Nepalese place that has lasted for decades and can count celebs among its regular customers.

The restaurant's location is another factor to take into account when choosing where to eat. Temple Bar is the city's tourist ghetto and there are places there that would go out of business in a week if the tourists disappeared. There are, however, also some excellent, stylish, if possibly overpriced, places that justify giving your credit card an airing. The area north of St Stephen's Green has some long-established but, again, pricey places, while Dawson Street is home to lots of café bars where you can eat, drink, chat and often listen to some live music. North of the river has always been a bit of a food desert but this, too, is improving with the new rejuvenated docks and IFSC area coming into their own.

Several of the city's restaurants have special menus, often called 'early bird', 'theatre' or just plain 'tourist' menus, which consist of a limited number of dishes from the evening à la carte available for an hour or two around 18.00–19.30 at reduced prices. If you want to eat early and not make a night of it, these can be a good option.

Finding a place for lunch is the least of your worries in the city. Most pubs make their profits from pub lunches and you are never more than a short walk from a pub in the city. The area around St Stephen's Green can become a bit fraught when the office workers

MAKING THE MOST OF DUBLIN

come out for lunch, while the further out of the centre you travel the less imaginative the pub lunch.

In summer, eating outside is always an option, especially if you have children in tow or are on a budget. Parks such as St Stephen's Green or Iveagh Gardens are open during daylight hours and are

◆ *Some traditional Irish goods*

EATING & DRINKING

free, and along the river there are lots of spots to sit and munch while people-watching. There are good delicatessen shops in the city centre and all supermarkets have ready-made sandwiches.

A strict smoking ban operates in all public buildings in Ireland, including pubs and restaurants (and hotel rooms). Most pubs have managed to find a little space in the open, euphemistically called a beer garden but more likely where they used to store the beer barrels. These are heated in winter by environmentally unfriendly gas braziers and often have an awning, so the nicotine-challenged can keep out of the rain. Lots of cafés have found space on the street for a similar arrangement.

The dress code in bars and restaurants is relaxed to say the least. Some very upmarket restaurants may ask men to wear a jacket, while clubs have a dress code which the bouncers seem to make up as the night and the queues outside progress but which generally involves the not-wearing of trainers.

Vegetarians will have a hard time of it in the city. There are few dedicated vegetarian restaurants and while most places have a veggie option, it's pretty much a lip service affair. Indian restaurants of course are always a good option, and fish-eating non-meat eaters will find themselves well catered for.

RESTAURANT CATEGORIES

Café and restaurant ratings in this book are based on the average price of a three-course dinner without drinks.

£ Budget	€20 or less
££ Mid-range	€21 to €45
£££ Most expensive	€46 plus

MAKING THE MOST OF DUBLIN

Entertainment & nightlife

Sometimes it seems there are two Dublins. There is the day-time, working city where rules are properly followed, red lights are obeyed, and opening and closing hours are adhered to. Then there is Friday-night and weekend Dublin, when the streets are reclaimed by those lost boys and girls who would like to be free spirits but just enjoy the cash-flow created by working for a living. For the young and healthy of liver, Dublin rocks from office-closing hours on Friday to winding down in a club on Sunday. Visitors can tap into this alcohol-fuelled weekend life of the Dubliners, although in Temple Bar and the city centre most nights throughout the week are also pretty lively till the early hours.

For those who want to live on the wild side, it is necessary to leave the rather corny music of Temple Bar and venture out. Try a pub crawl along South Great George Street starting at the top of the street in Hogan's or the Globe, calling in at the Long Hall, working your way down to the Bleeding Horse from where you can swing over to one of the clubs in Harcourt Street, Wexford Street or Leeson Street.

There are good places to hear live music of all descriptions in the city, from the stuff they churn out in Temple Bar for the tourists to some excellent small pubs which offer traditional musicians or good local rock music, or places like The Point where megastars of all descriptions fill up what was once a train depot, and which some say never recovered. Good places to check out what's on are some of the music stores or pubs that serve food during the day. Papers such as the free *Event Guide*, the monthly *Slate* or the glossy *In Dublin*, will

◗ *The highly popular Temple Bar pub*

MAKING THE MOST OF DUBLIN

give a good idea of what's happening in a city where clubs go out of fashion as quickly as last year's platform soles. All are available free from cafés, newsagents and hotels.

If it's a hooley you're looking for, there are several places which put on Irish traditional dance and music shows, a kind of amalgam of Riverdance and real Irish dancing. The Arlington Hotel in Bachelors Walk (01 804 9100) has nightly music and dance shows, and two places out of town are also worth checking out: Johnnie Fox's (Glencullen 01 295 5647) does hooley nights which include dinner and the show; and Taylor's Three Rock (Grange Rd, Rathfarnham 01 494 2999 www.TaylorsIrishNight.com) organises a shuttle bus from the city centre, again offering dinner and a show.

Considering the number of stand-up comics which Ireland has produced, the city has few really good stand-up venues, although a few places have one or two nights dedicated to comedy. Again,

ENTERTAINMENT & NIGHTLIFE

check the listings since these places change frequently, but good places to seek out are the Ha'penny Bridge (see page 84), The International (see page 72) and The Sugar Club (see page 73). In 2006 Murphy's Laughter Lounge (see page 98) reopened after several years of reconstruction, although whether its shows justify its high admission charge remains to be seen.

Movie-lovers will enjoy the city. There are the usual range of multi-screen theatres (see 'When it rains'), but also the Irish Film Centre (ⓐ 6 Eustace St ⓣ 01 679 3477 ⓦ www.fii.ie), which shows independent, foreign and documentary films, and Screen (ⓐ D'Olier St ⓣ 01 672 5500), which shows a mixture of arthouse and mainstream movies. Dublin has two film festivals (see pages 9, 10) and in summer movies are shown in the open air at Meeting House Square.

⬇ *Experience the essence of the Irish here*

MAKING THE MOST OF DUBLIN

Sport & relaxation

SPECTATOR SPORTS
Football
Shamrock Rovers ⓐ Spawell Leisure Complex ⓣ 01 492 5660

Gaelic Football
Gaelic football is played by 15 strong teams who can handle the ball as well as kick it. It is probably closer to rugby than football. Amateur games are played in **Phoenix Park** (ⓐ Parkgate St, near Castleknock ⓣ 01 677 0095) at weekends, but **Croke Park** is the main stadium (ⓐ Jones Rd, Drumcondra ⓣ 01 836 3222 ⓦ www.gaa.ie). The stadium has a museum with displays on the history of the place and the game. The stadium was the scene of an attack on spectators by the British Black and Tans during the war for independence.

Greyhound racing
Harold's Cross Racetrack ⓐ 151 Harold's Cross Rd ⓣ 01 479 1081
ⓣ 20.00 Mon, Tues & Fri; admission charge
Shelbourne Park Stadium ⓐ Lotts Rd, Ringsend ⓣ 01 668 3502
ⓣ 20.00 Wed, Thur & Sat

Horse racing
Leopardstown Racetrack, Foxrock ⓣ 01 2839 3607
ⓦ www.leopardstown.com ⓣ 23 meetings a year; dates on website
ⓑ Bus: Éireann operates a special race day bus service (ⓣ 01 873 4222)

Rugby
Lansdowne Road Stadium 14 domestic teams play for the Leinster Senior Cup and the Six Nations games are played here. The stadium

SPORT & RELAXATION

will be closed for a time during 2007 for redevelopment, and games will be played at Croke Park. ❶ 01 668 4601

PARTICIPATION SPORTS
Bowling
Leisureplex ⓐ Malahide Rd, Coolock ❶ 01 848 5722;
ⓐ Blanchardstown ❶ 01 822 3030; ⓐ Stillorgan ❶ 01 288 1656

Jogging
Jogging in the city's parks is a safe activity during daylight hours. Phoenix Park (see page 104), Iveagh Gardens, the Grand Canal towpaths, and Herbert Park in Ballsbridge, all make good locations for jogging.

Swimming
National Aquatic Centre ⓐ Snugborough Rd, Blanchardstown ❶ 01 646 300 ⓦ www.nac.ie ⓑ 14.00–20.45 Mon–Fri, 09.00–19.45 Sat & Sun

Tennis
There are tennis courts for hire in the following parks:
Albert College Park ⓐ Glasnevin ❶ 01 837 3891
Bushy Park ⓐ Terenure ❶ 01 490 0320
Eamonn Ceannt Park ⓐ Crumlin ❶ 01 454 0799
Herbert Park ⓐ Ballsbridge ❶ 01 668 4364

Water sports
Sea Safari offers boat trips in a rigid inflatable around Dublin Bay. Lifejackets are supplied. ⓐ Malahide Village Marina or Dublin City Moorings ❶ 01 806 1626 ⓦ www.seasafari.ie

MAKING THE MOST OF DUBLIN

Accommodation

Dublin has accommodation ranging from super exclusive boutique hotels to dorm beds in hostels and all of them are very much in demand in the high season or when a big event is on in the city, so you are best to book before you arrive. As the city becomes wealthier, more top-end hotels are appearing, and budget places upgrade to get the most out of the booming tourist trade. The most luxurious places are, generally speaking, south of the river around Merrion Square, St Stephen's Green and further out in Ballsbridge. The O'Connell Street area has the majority of budget hotels and guesthouse accommodation. Its advantage over Ballsbridge is its central location. Its disadvantage is that it can get noisy at night. Temple Bar is rapidly becoming a little enclave for party-going. It is possible to spend a weekend in Temple Bar and never leave. Its hotels are good 3-star quality, but like O'Connell Street, the area can be noisy at night.

Abbey Hotel £ Small, comfortable hotel with its own car park.
ⓐ 52 Middle Abbey St ⓣ 01 872 8188
ⓦ www.abbey-hotel.com

Avalon House Hostel £ If price is your main priority, this place is for you. Single and double rooms in a well-run hostel. Book early and be prepared for lots of noise. ⓐ 55 Aungier St ⓣ 01 475 0001
ⓦ www.avalon-house.ie

Bewleys Hotel Ballsbridge £ Probably the best value in the city, a 3-star hotel with 1-star rates. Great restaurant too. ⓐ Merrion Rd, Ballsbridge ⓣ 01 668 1111 ⓦ www.bewleyshotels.com

ACCOMMODATION

The Brewery Hostel £ Out of the main tourist area, this is a quiet place with private rooms as well as dorm beds.
ⓐ 22–23 Thomas St ⓣ 01 453 8600 ⓦ www.irish-hostel.com

Days Inn Talbot St £ One of a chain of budget guesthouses. Small basic rooms but good value. ⓐ 95–98 Talbot St ⓣ 01 874 9202
ⓦ www.daysinntalbot.com

Four Courts Hostel £ South of the river and opposite the Four Courts this has some basic but clean private rooms as well as dormitories. Kitchen, pool table, reading area, internet access. ⓐ 15–17 Merchant's Quay ⓣ 01 672 5839 ⓦ www.fourcourtshostel.com

Hazelbrook House £ Large guesthouse in a street full of good value, budget accommodation. Facilities compare with some of the city's hotels. ⓐ 85 Lower Gardiner St ⓣ 01 836 5003
ⓦ www.hazelbrookhouse.ie

Jurys Inn Christchurch £ Big, functional place which charges a room rate – great if you have children. Good location, out of the hubbub but close to the sights. ⓐ Christchurch Place ⓣ 01 454 0000
ⓦ www.jurysinns.com

Jurys Inn Croke Park £ Shiny new hotel with a sporty theme. Everything you could ask for in a room plus internet access. ⓐ Croke Park Stadium, Jones's Rd ⓣ 01 871 4444 ⓦ www.jurysdoyle.com/crokepark

Jury's Inn Custom House £ Another branch of the good value chain of hotels. Room rate covers up to three adults or family of four.
ⓐ Custom House Quay ⓣ 01 607 5000 ⓦ www.jurysinns.com

MAKING THE MOST OF DUBLIN

> **ACCOMMODATION RATINGS**
> Hotel, guesthouse and hostel ratings are based on the average price of a double room per night in high season, including breakfast:
> £ Budget   €90 or less
> ££ Mid-range   €91 to €200
> £££ Most expensive   €201 plus

Kelly's Hotel £ Small, family-owned and family-run hotel in a good location for all the sights and nightlife. ⓐ 36 South Great George's St ⓣ 01 677 9277 ⓦ www.kellyshtl.com

Kinlay House Christchurch £ Private rooms with shared or en suite bathrooms in this hostel. Laundry and kitchen make up for the lack of luxuries. ⓐ 2–12 Lord Edward St ⓣ 01 679 6644 ⓦ www.kinlayhouse.ie

Oliver St John Gogarty £ Smart hostel with private rooms, safe, kitchens, laundry, internet access. ⓐ 18–21 Anglesea St ⓣ 01 671 1822 ⓦ www.gogartys.ie

Phoenix Park House £ Small, family-run guesthouse close to Phoenix Park. Bus ride into the city centre. Lots of facilities and a good bargain. ⓐ 38–39 Parkgate St ⓣ 01 677 2870 ⓦ www.dublinguesthouse.com

Best Western Academy Hotel £–££ Located in a quiet street off O'Connell Street with all the facilities of a good 3-star hotel. Free wireless internet connection too. ⓐ Findlater Place ⓣ 01 878 0666 ⓦ www.academyhotel.ie

ACCOMMODATION

Best Western Ashling Hotel £–££ Small busy place, a good way out of the city centre but close to a good bus route. ⓐ Parkgate St ⓘ 01677 2324 ⓦ www.bestwesternashlinghotel.ie

Mespil Hotel £–££ Big, modern hotel on the bank of the Grand Canal, well out of the noise and bustle of Dublin's nightlife. ⓐ Mespil Rd ⓘ 01 488 4600 ⓦ www.leehotels.com

Blooms ££ Very centrally located hotel with its own nightclub, this place would suit party-goers. Pleasant rooms in a busy place. ⓐ 6 Anglesea St ⓘ 01 671 5622 ⓦ www.blooms.ie

◓ *Dining at the Jurys Inn Croke Park Hotel*

MAKING THE MOST OF DUBLIN

Camden Court Hotel ££ Large, purpose-built hotel right in the heart of nightclub territory. Close enough to sights, and offering a pool and fitness centre. ⓐ Camden St ⓣ 01 475 9666
ⓦ www.camdencourthotel.ie

Egan's House Hotel ££ Small, comfortable and friendly guesthouse in quiet, suburban location close to the Botanic Gardens. An excellent choice if all the palaver of the city gets you down.
ⓐ 7 Iona Park, Glasnevin ⓣ 01 830 3611
ⓦ www.eganshouse.com

Morrison Hotel ££ A fashionable boutique hotel with the kind of luxurious atmosphere that makes you want to stay in and order room service. It has a spa and an excellent restaurant. ⓐ Lower Ormond Quay ⓣ 01 887 2400 ⓦ www.morrisonhotel.ie

Paramount Hotel ££ A busy hotel deep in the heart of Temple Bar but one which has rooms overlooking a central courtyard so the potential noise doesn't filter through. Breakfast, in the Turk's Head bar downstairs, can get busy too, so eat early. Plus, it's not far to walk or taxi home after a night out. ⓐ Parliament St and Essex Gate
ⓣ 01 417 9900 ⓦ www.paramounthotel.ie

The Park Inn ££ Modern, breezy hotel with a good bar and some live music sessions. Large, airy rooms with lots of facilities. ⓐ Smithfield Village ⓣ 01 817 3838 ⓦ www.hoteldirect.co.uk/dublin

The Clarence £££ There just aren't enough pound signs to cover the rates at this stylish place, which is owned by Bono and The Edge of U2 fame. Leather lifts, over the top luxury in the rooms. Nice bar and

ACCOMMODATION

restaurant and the occasional celebrity. 🅐 6–8 Wellington Quay 🅣 01 407 0800 🅦 www.theclarence.ie

Clarion Hotel £££ Set in the IFSC area, this purpose-built, well-designed place is right on the riverfront, close to O'Connell Street and surrounded by the sandwich bars and cafés of the business district. Fitness centre, pool, nice bar food, good breakfast. 🅐 Excise Walk 🅣 01 433 8800 🅦 www.clarionhotelifsc.com

🔺 *Enjoy a hearty breakfast at Egan's House Hotel*

THE BEST OF DUBLIN

Whether you are on a flying visit to Dublin, or taking a more leisurely break, there are some sights that should not be missed.

TOP 10 ATTRACTIONS

- *The Book of Kells* Exquisite medieval illustrated manuscript housed in an excellent exhibition within Trinity College's Old Library (see page 60).

- **Christ Church Cathedral** Beautiful, medieval, mosaic floors, the tomb of Strongbow and a crypt full of treasures (see page 76).

- **St Patrick's Cathedral** The ancient rival to Christchurch where the Duke of Kildare chanced his arm (see page 109).

- **Guinness Storehouse** Panoramic views of the city and a pint of stout as well (see page 103).

- **A walk around Howth Head** Wheeling seabirds, rare plant life, old lighthouses and a bracing afternoon's walk ends up in the pretty seaside town of Howth (see page 116).

- **National Museum of Archaeology and History** Find out about Ireland's troubled past (see page 66).

- **A pub crawl down South Great George Street to Camden Street** Start early, stop for dinner then head south where the evenings get wilder (see page 70).

- **Francis Bacon's Studio at the Hugh Lane Gallery** This guy really had tidying-up issues. The studio, relocated from London, gives incredible and vivid insight into the artist's life, work and techniques (see page 91).

- **Malahide Castle** Find out how the wealthy landowners lived and maybe encounter the castle's ghost (see page 119).

- **A boat ride on the Liffey** or take the Viking Splash Tour. Throw self-respect and decorum to the wind, put on the daft Viking helmet and enjoy (see page 151).

Four Courts: a truly awesome sight

MAKING THE MOST OF DUBLIN

Your at-a-glance guide to seeing the best Dublin has to offer, depending on how much time you have.

HALF-DAY: DUBLIN IN A HURRY
With a half day in Dublin the place to head for is the Guinness Storehouse where you can see the entire city in one go. From there head back to Temple Bar for an alfresco lunch while taking in the ambience.

1 DAY: TIME TO SEE A LITTLE MORE
With an entire day at your disposal, there is time to take in a couple more of the big sights, namely *The Book of Kells* or the National Museum of Archaeology and History with its displays of gold and the history of Dublin's strangest time, the 1916 Uprising. Consider a picnic lunch in St Stephen's Green feeding the ducks and watching Dubliners taking a break. In the afternoon you could hit the

△ *Watching over the River Liffey*

THE BEST OF DUBLIN

Guinness Storehouse or, if stout doesn't appeal, climb St Michael's Tower for slightly smudgier but equally fascinating views. For dinner try Monty's of Kathmandu (see page 81) in Temple Bar or perhaps Eliza Blue's (see page 81) with its views across the river and then just join in the fun of Temple Bar, drifting as people do from one bar to the next and ending the night in one of the area's clubs.

2–3 DAYS: SHORT CITY BREAK
The two great ancient churches are worth visiting, and you will also have time to venture into north Dublin to visit Phoenix Park, the Writer's Museum and the Hugh Lane Gallery, and wander around the shopping streets of Henry Street, Moore Street and their tiny malls and department stores. A day out on the DART is possible either to Howth in the north or Dun Laoghaire and points south, following the coastline on the now ancient railway line. The nights can be filled with the glories of Temple Bar, a wander down the watering holes of South Great George Street, or one of the many guided tours of ancient pubs. Venture out to Cobblestone (see page 113) for some authentic traditional music and try a meal at One Pico (see page 70) for a special night out.

LONGER: ENJOYING DUBLIN TO THE FULL
With more time to spend, you can enjoy a leisurely wander around the National Gallery or venture out to the Collins Barracks, one of the biggest army barracks in Europe and now home to a branch of the National Museum. Your day trip could extend to Skerries, a genuine seaside town with thatched roofs, a summer fun-fair and some elegant, great houses to explore. Best of all, consider taking one of the trips out to Newgrange Passage Tomb, a Neolithic wonder of engineering.

MAKING THE MOST OF DUBLIN

Something for nothing

Some of the best things to do in Dublin don't cost a penny. Several of the museums have no entry charge and are listed below, but the city itself is a sight to behold, with its intact Georgian squares such as Merrion Square or Mountjoy Square, where you can admire the elegant architectural details of the buildings. Lots of the squares have little parks which can afford you an hour or so of pleasant relaxation in the middle of your sightseeing day. Christchurch and St Patrick's Cathedral have no admission charge, and if you enjoy churches you can visit the Carmelite Church in Whitefriar Street where St Valentine's bones are kept, or St Mary's Abbey in Meetinghouse Lane, a medieval chapter house with an exhibition of medieval life (⏱ 09.30–17.00 Wed & Sat mid-June–mid-Sept).

If you discount the cost of the DART fare, a day trip out to the seaside at Bray will cost you nothing and neither will the most amazing cliff walk you've ever experienced around Bray Head. The cliff walk at Howth, too, costs nothing, and doing a day or so of the Wicklow Way is a rewarding if strenuous way to not spend any money.

You could also spend a day seeking out all the city's statuary, go and find the bullet holes in the statue of O'Connell at O'Connell Bridge, or stand out in the street in Temple Bar and listen to some of the music coming from inside the pubs.

All of the following have free admission:

Carmelite Church ⓐ 56 Aungier St
Chester Beatty Library (see page 76)
Dublin City Gallery (see page 91)
St Audoen's Church Medieval parish church and exhibition on the life of St Audoen. ⓐ Cornmarket, High St ⓞ 01 677 0088
⏱ 09.30–17.30 June–Sept

SOMETHING FOR NOTHING

Iveagh Gardens Secluded park in the centre of town, with waterfall, grotto, maze and archery grounds. ⓐ Clonmel St
Irish Jewish Museum (see page 104)
Irish Museum of Modern Art (see page 105)
National Botanic Gardens 19.5 hectares (48 acres) of beautiful glasshouses and rare plants. ⓐ Glasnevin ⓣ 01 804 0300
ⓞ 09.00–18.00 Mon–Sat, 10.00–16.30 Sun (till dusk in winter)
ⓑ Bus: 13, 19 (from O'Connell St), 134 (from Middle Abbey St)
National Gallery (see page 64)
National Museum of Archaeology and History (see page 65)
National Museum of Decorative Arts & History at Collins Barracks (see page 106)
National Museum of Natural History (see page 65)
National Photographic Archive (see page 78)

▲ *Visit the Georgian houses by the seaside in Bray*

MAKING THE MOST OF DUBLIN

When it rains

The advent of rain in Dublin is barely noticed by its citizens, who just get out their umbrellas and carry on with what they were doing. For the visitor it might limit what you can do – Howth Head wouldn't be too much fun and neither would the Wicklow Way. But the city has lots of indoor activities. Shopping will keep you out of the rain for hours, especially if you keep to the malls and big department stores. Another option is The City Sightseeing Tour (❶ 01 605 7705, admission charge) is a hop-on, hop-off live commentary tour of the city which takes you to 20 different sights and will keep you dry in between sights (as long as you don't sit in the open-top upper deck). The buses are located outside the GPO in O'Connell Street and leave at 15 minute intervals.

The National Museum of Archaeology and History with its hoards of gold, the National Gallery with its Picasso and Caravaggio, and the National Museum of Natural History, filled with things pickled in alcohol, are all a quick dash away from each other and would could easily fill a whole day. Another cluster of sights is Christ Church Cathedral, the Dublinia exhibition and St Michael's Tower, which you can climb to the top to see if the clouds are breaking. Movie-watching always makes a good keeping-dry activity, and there are cinemas in Eustace Street (❶ 01 679 3477), O'Connell Street (ⓐ The Savoy ❶ 01 878 8487), D'Olier Street (see page 31), and Parnell Street (ⓐ UGC ❶ 01 872 8444). Indoor sports also make a good activity for a rainy day. Consider visiting a pool (see page 30) or going bowling (see page 33). You might consider taking the DART out to Malahide; it's a pleasant journey and you can hop straight out of the train and into Malahide Castle. The tour is excellent and afterwards there are other sights to visit inside the castle courtyard.

WHEN IT RAINS

Best of all on a rainy day perhaps is to find a warm café bar, say Bewley's Café Bar (see page 69) and linger over a coffee or something stronger while you smugly watch the people outside getting wet.

🔺 *Take a break at the Chester Beatty Library café*

MAKING THE MOST OF DUBLIN

On arrival

TIME DIFFERENCES
Ireland is on GMT. During Daylight Saving Time (late Mar–late Sept), the clocks are put ahead one hour. At 12.00 in Dublin in the middle of summer, times elsewhere are as follows:
Australia Eastern Standard Time 21.00, Central Standard Time 20.30, Western Standard Time 19.00
New Zealand 23.00
South Africa 13.00
UK 12.00
USA and **Canada** Newfoundland Time 08.30, Atlantic Canada Time 08.00, Eastern Time 07.00, Central Time 06.00, Mountain Time 05.00, Pacific Time 04.00, Alaska 03.00

ARRIVING
By air
Dublin Airport (❶ 01 844 4900) is 12 km (7½ miles) north of the city. Its arrival hall has a tourist office (see page 155) which can book accommodation, money exchange facilities, left luggage, cash machines, car hire booths, and a CIE counter which will provide information on bus services. If you plan to hire a car you should do so before you leave your own country since there can be shortages in the summer. The journey into the city is by bus or taxi. There is no train service.

Buses
Dublin Bus runs two bus services called the Airlink Express. The 747 travels directly to O'Connell Street, then to the central bus station (Busáras ❸ Store St ❶ 01 836 6111 ⓦ www.buseireann.ie) and

ON ARRIVAL

Connolly Station. The 748 takes in Tara St DART station, Aston Quay (for Temple Bar) and Heuston Station (for destinations in the south of the country). CIE sells prepaid tickets, single or return, or you can pay the bus driver. Both buses pick up passengers directly outside the entrance to the arrivals hall. ❶ 01 873 4222 ❿ www.dublinbus.ie ❿ the 747 runs every 15 minutes 05.45–23.30 Mon–Sat, 07.15–23.30 Sun; the 748 departs every 30 minutes 06.25–21.30 Mon–Sat, 07.05–22.30 Sun

⬤ *A sightseeing tour is always a good way to see the city*

MAKING THE MOST OF DUBLIN

ON ARRIVAL

MAKING THE MOST OF DUBLIN

The privately run **Aircoach** runs to Merrion Square and into Ballsbridge, stopping at designated points. It is useful for visitors staying south of the river. It picks up passengers in the access road in front of the arrivals hall. ❶ 01 844 7118 Ⓦ www.aircoach.ie ⏰ every 15 minutes 05.30–23.30

Another alternative is to use the **regular public bus**, numbers 41 and 41B to Eden Quay, or 16 and 16A to Aungier Street. They are less expensive but take much longer. They are useful for visitors staying in the north of the city.

Taxis
Taxis are metered and readily available outside the arrivals hall. The cost will depend on traffic conditions but should be about €25.

By ferry
Dun Laoghaire The Stena ferry docks at Dun Laoghaire (❶ 01 204 7700) from where foot passengers can take the DART or bus 7, 7A or 8 into the city. Drivers will find the route into the city signposted.
Dublin Port Bus 53 meets incoming ferries. Its destination is the central bus station. Taxis are also available.

By train
Trains from Rosslaire, Belfast and towns in Northern Ireland arrive at **Connolly Station** (ⓐ Amiens St ❶ 01 836 3333 Ⓦ www.irishrail.ie). Connolly has left luggage facilities, connects with the DART and with Busáras via bus 90 from outside the station. There are also taxis available.

Trains from Cork, Galway, Westport, Tralee, Killarney, Limerick, Wexford and Waterford arrive at **Heuston Station** (ⓐ St John's Rd West ❶ 01 836 5421 Ⓦ www.irishrail.ie) in the west of the city.

ON ARRIVAL

Heuston has left luggage facilities, ATM machines, shops and cafés and connects with the city centre via bus 90 and several local buses.

By road

Long-distance buses arrive at Busáras (see page 48) from destinations around the country and from Northern Ireland. There are seven daily arrivals and departures from Belfast. Journey time is about three hours. Car drivers from Northern Ireland will arrive in the north of the city via the M1 motorway. Be aware that parking in the city is at a premium and most hotels do not have their own car parks.

FINDING YOUR FEET

Dublin is as safe a city as you can expect in Western Europe, perhaps a little safer than most. Drug crime has increased and there is always the risk of mugging or bag snatching. ATM machines have entered the criminal repertoire with sophisticated gadgets reading PINs as they are keyed in, so choose an ATM in a public place and check that it doesn't look tampered with. Bear in mind, though, that while there are gun crimes reported on Irish radio on a weekly basis, this is because Ireland is a small country and there is little other news. It is common to hear on national radio news of a fight in Galway, for instance, where no one was seriously injured or arrested, or a car accident where someone was slightly injured.

    For the newly arrived visitor to Ireland the chief problem with settling into the pace of life, even in Dublin, is learning to slow down. Hotels and B&Bs do breakfast often until 10.30, smaller shops and cafés open at 09.30 or later, and most of the museums get

MAKING THE MOST OF DUBLIN

going at around 10.00. A major activity in the city is talking; complete strangers will gossip away at bus stops and your cab driver will lecture you on Dublin politics or winkle out of you all your family history, your Irish roots, where you've come from and where you're going. Where other cities offer great sights, art works or beautiful architecture as their main attractions, Dublin's greatest offer is its citizens, and to really enjoy life in Dublin you have to take the time to stop and chat wherever possible.

ORIENTATION

The city is divided rather neatly in two by the Liffey River, and to avoid confusion it is as well to bear in mind the compass points when travelling around. In the north of the city the central street is O'Connell Street. North of this is Parnell Square and to the west of it is Smithfield and Phoenix Park. To the east of O'Connell Street is the new IFSC (International Financial Services Centre), Custom House and hotels along the river, and further east is The Point depot, then the river estuary.

The south of the river is dominated by Westmoreland Street and Grafton Street. To their west is the area known as the Liberties, where you can visit the Guinness Storehouse, the National Gallery of Modern Art and Kilmainham Gaol. East of the main thoroughfare are Temple Bar, Trinity College and Merrion Square. To the south of Grafton Street is the Grand Canal and beyond that Ballsbridge, where much of the accommodation can be found.

To the north of Dublin along the coastline of Dublin Bay is first Howth, then Malahide, then Skerries, all accessible by DART or suburban rail. To the south is Dun Laoghaire, Bray and then County Wicklow.

ON ARRIVAL

Iarnród Éireann
- Kildare
- Northern
- Southeastern
- Western
- DART

Luas
- Red
- Green

- Airlink 747
- Airlink 748

- Stena Sealink / Irish Ferries

← Aston Quay — stops only in direction shown

Dundalk *Dún Dealgan*
Balbriggan *Baile Brigín*
Skerries *Na Sceirí*
Rush & Lusk *An Ros & Lusca*
Donabate *Domhnach Bat*
Malahide *Mullach Íde*
Portmarnock *Port Mearnóg*

Howth *Binn Éadair*
Sutton *Cill Fhiontáin*
Bayside *Cois Bá*
Howth Junction *Cabhal Bhinn Éadair*
Kilbarrack *Cill Bharróg*
Raheny *Ráth Eanaigh*
Harmonstown *Baile Hearman*
Killester *Cill Easra*
Clontarf Road *Bóthar Chluain Tarbh*

Dublin Airport *Aerfort Átha Cliath* (747)(748)

Longford *An Longfort*
Maynooth *Maigh Nuad*
Leixlip Louisa Bridge *Léim an Bhradáin Droichead Louisa*
Leixlip Confey *Léim an Bhradáin Confaí*
Clonsilla *Cluain Saileach*
Coolmine *Cúil Mín*
Ashtown *Bhaile Ás*
Castleknock *Caisleán Cnucha*
Drumcondra *Droim Conrach*
Broombridge *Droichead na Scuab*

(747) **Busáras** *Busáras*
Connolly Station *Stáisiún Uí Chonghaile*

Museum *Ard-Mhúsaem*
Smithfield *Margadh na Feirme*
The Four Courts *Na Ceithre Cúirteanna*
Jervis *Jervis*
Abbey Street *Sráid na Mainistreach*

Tara Street *Sráid na Teamhrach*
Pearse Station *Stáisiún na bPiarsach*

Kildare *Cill Dara*
Heuston *Heuston* (748)
St Stephen's Green *Faiche Stiabhna*

James's *Ospidéal San Séamas*
Fatima *Fatima*
Rialto *Rialto*
Suir Road *Bóthar na Siúire*
Goldenbridge *An Droichead Órga*
Drimnagh *Droimeanach*
Blackhorse *An Capall Dubh*
Bluebell *An Cloigín Gorm*
Kylemore *An Chill Mhór*
Red Cow *An Bhó Dhearg*
Kingswood *Coill an Rí*
Belgard *Belgard*
Cookstown *Baile an Chócaigh*
Hospital *Ospidéal Thamhlachta*
Tallaght *Tamhlacht*

Harcourt *Sráid Fhearchair*
Charlemont *Charlemont*
Ranelagh *Raghnallach*
Beechwood *Bóthar Choill na Feá*
Cowper *Cowper*
Milltown *Baile an Mhuilinn*
Windy Arbour *Na Glasáin*
Dundrum *Dún Droma*
Balally *Baile Amhlaoibh*
Kilmacud *Cill Mochuda*
Stillorgan *Stigh Lorgan*
Sandyford *Áth an Ghainimh*

Grand Canal Dock *Dug an Canálach Móire*
Lansdowne Road *Bóthar Lansdún*
Sandymount *Dumhach Thrá*
Sydney Parade *Paráid Sydney*
Booterstown *Baile an Bhóthair*
Blackrock *An Charraig Dhubh*
Seapoint *Rinn na Mara*
Salthill & Monkstown *Cnoc an tSalainn & Baile na Manach*
Dún Laoghaire *Dún Laoghaire*
Sandycove & Glasthule *Cuas an Ghainimh agus Tuathail*
Glenageary *Gleann na gCaorach*
Greystones *Na Clocha Liatha*
Gorey *Guaire*

Holyhead

IRISH SEA

A Communicarta Style 45 design
Map user: WZFG/CS/DUB/2006/18/4
© Communicarta Ltd, 6/2006 UDN.5

MAKING THE MOST OF DUBLIN

GETTING AROUND

Dublin is a compact city and the majority of sights and attractions as well as shopping areas can be reached on foot. If your accommodation is outside the city centre or if you want to get to some of the outlying sights, you'll find the bus service is inexpensive and efficient while the Luas tram system, less useful within the city, is an interesting experience.

Bus

Dublin Bus stops are painted green and usually have a timetable posted on them. The driver is paid on entry with the exact fare in coins. If you are uncertain as to the fare, the driver will tell you. If you don't have the exact change the driver will issue a receipt for the excess money and you can reclaim it at Dublin Bus in O'Connell Street.

There are several concessionary tickets which will make travelling around the city easier and slightly cheaper. The rambler ticket allows unlimited bus travel for 1, 3, 5 or 7 days. With a photo ID from Dublin Bus there are also concessionary tickets allowing a combination of bus and DART travel or bus and Luas, but unless you are staying for some time and intend to travel around the city a lot, they may not be worth the expense. There are also Family Bus Travel tickets allowing unlimited family travel on buses and DART. For details on all passes and other information, check www.dublinbus.ie. Another option to consider is the Dublin Pass, offering free access to some tourist attractions, discounts in some cafés and shops and free transport on the Aircoach airport bus. You'd have to work hard,

> Statue of Molly Malone, the legendary fishmonger

though, to get your money's worth. The pass can be bought online at www.dublinpass.ie

Luas

These trams are really for commuters but you could use it to get out to Collins Barracks and Smithfield and it's good fun. Tickets are bought at the stops from the machines. Singles are valid for an hour and return tickets last the day they are purchased.
Ⓦ www.luas.ie

Train

The DART and suburban rail services travel along the coast to Skerries, Malahide, Howth, Dun Laoghaire and Bray, among other destinations. Tickets can be bought at the stations. DART stations in the city are Tara Street, Connolly Station and Pearse Street. The last DART trains out of Bray and Howth run at about midnight.

Taxis

Taxi ranks are at St Stephen's Green, College Green and O'Connell Street.

Car & cycle hire

Road driving or cycling around the city is not recommended. Traffic in the city is either far too fast for comfort or completely gridlocked at rush hours, and parking during weekdays will take up most of your time and cash. Few city hotels have car parks of their own so overnight parking can really put up your costs. There are no cycle lanes and few places where cycles can be left safely.

◐ *The Famine Memorial: a constant reminder of hardships past*

THE CITY OF Dublin

THE CITY

Grafton Street & surrounding area

While the area north of the river spent the late 20th century sinking into decay and pound shops, the south side has always flourished. At its epicentre is Grafton Street, home to posh department stores and British chain stores. Settled all around is the seat of government, the big museums, some very exclusive hotels, St Stephen's Green and the fabulously expensive Georgian terraces of Merrion Square and its surrounds. Further south is the long road that starts off as South Great George Street, turns into Camden Street and becomes Wexford Street. This area has more pubs than you can shake a stick at. If you had only a couple of days in the city, there would be no need to venture across the river; most of what you want to see is tucked into this area and its tourist-dominated neighbour, Temple Bar.

SIGHTS & ATTRACTIONS

Bank of Ireland
Not normally on the must-see list for a visit to a city, this bank was once the old parliament building and still contains intact the Irish House of Lords, complete with tapestries, mace and all the other paraphernalia of Irish Protestant home rule.
ⓐ College Green ⓘ 01 677 6801 ⓛ tours at 10.30, 11.30 & 13.45 Tues

The Book of Kells
Housed in the Old Library, a repository of three million or so books, *The Book of Kells* is a 9th-century illustrated manuscript of the four gospels. It had a turbulent life before it arrived in Trinity; robbed from the island of Iona by marauding Vikings, the book lost its

Grafton Street & surrounding area

0 — 400 metres
0 — 400 yards

THE CITY

probably gold- and precious-stone-clad bindings and several of the outer pages. You view the manuscript itself inside a tiny glass case in a darkened room after wandering through an excellent exhibition on its manufacture and history. Afterwards you can wander through the rest of the library admiring the impressive collection housed here.

ⓐ Old Library, Trinity College ⓣ 01 608 2320 ⓦ www.tcd.ie/library ⓛ 09.30–17.00 Mon–Sat, 09.30–16.30 Sun (May–Sept); 09.30–17.00 Mon–Sat, 12.00–16.30 Sun, closed for 10 days over Christmas (Oct–Apr); admission charge

Merrion Square

Home to some of the most expensive real estate in the city, Merrion Square, built in 1762, was always where the really cool people lived, as you can see from the surfeit of blue plaques on the houses. Most famously, Oscar Wilde lived here with his parents and this is commemorated inside the little park with an ornate statue affectionately known to locals as 'the queer with the sneer' (look at his expression) or 'the queer in the square' (it rhymes if you say it in a Dublin accent).

Newman House

These two Georgian buildings, home for a time to the Catholic University, are open to the public for guided tours only during the summer. The tour includes Gerard Manley Hopkins' rooms (he taught here in the final years of his life), the Apollo Room, where the glorious stucco plaster of the Lanfranchi brothers has been brought back to its original state, and a restored saloon where the Georgian gentry would once have played host to their friends.

ⓐ 85–86 St Stephen's Green ⓣ 01 716 7422 ⓛ tours at 12.00, 14.00,

GRAFTON STREET & SURROUNDING AREA

15.00 & 16.00 Tues & Fri (June–Aug); admission charge ⓝ Bus: 7, 10, 45; DART: Pearse St

Number 29
If you enjoy Georgiana then this more modest Georgian home is fun to visit. Research has turned up the original owners of the house and the tour includes details of their life, including the fascinating upstairs-downstairs relationship. The whole house is furnished in stuff from the archives of the National Museum, so it looks just as the original family would have had it.
ⓐ 29 Fitzwilliam St Lower ⓣ 01 702 6165 ⓦ www.esb.ie/education
ⓛ 10.00–17.00 Tues–Sat, 13.00–17.00 Sun, closed for 2 weeks before Christmas; admission charge ⓝ Bus: 7, 10, 45; DART: Pearse St

St Stephen's Green
If one part of the city can be said to summarise Dublin's existence, it is St Stephen's Green. Public grazing area, public hanging site, home to the strolling middle classes, site of one of the fiercest battles of the 1916 Uprising and now repository of all the commemorative detritus of several hundred years of fighting. There is also a nice park with a duck pond and benches where you can enjoy a picnic. Seek out the bust of Countess Markeivicz, one of the few unsung women heroes of the Uprising.

Trinity College
Established by Queen Elizabeth I in an effort to keep the young and impressionable sons of the Protestant ascendancy away from the vices of Europe, Trinity was for centuries a little bastion of Protestant education. Until 1970 the Catholic church actually forbade Catholic students from attending the place. Inside the

THE CITY

gates is a little haven of quiet learning (or it would be, except for the students and the hordes of tourists visiting the Book of Kells). Admire the architecture (most of which is Georgian rather than Elizabethan) and lovely squares, but follow the crowds to the real draw, the Book of Kells. The Dublin Experience, a multimedia presentation on the history of the city, is in the Arts Building here. It's fairly missable, unless you like that sort of thing.

Trinity College ⓐ College Green ⓣ 01 608 2320 ⓦ www.tcd.ie
The Dublin Experience ⓐ Arts Building, Trinity College
ⓛ 10.00–19.00 May–Oct; admission charge

CULTURE

National Gallery

Considering how small and poor Ireland was until the 1990s (it couldn't take in a single Jewish refugee during World War II), this

> **SHEILA NA GIGS**
>
> In medieval times it was common for carved stone female figures to be inserted over the side doors of churches. These figures were seriously ugly, pulling wild faces and exposing their genitals to whomever looked up. One theory for this strange creature, the Sheila na gig, is that she was there to frighten off evil-doers from the church. Perhaps she stood as a warning to women to behave themselves. In more prudish times the Sheila na gigs were taken down from the church doorways and two of them have found their way into the room at the National Museum of Archaeology and History which holds the famous gold Ardagh Chalice.

GRAFTON STREET & SURROUNDING AREA

collection is quite impressive. Its contents are strong on Italian art, with Mantegna, Titian, Tintoretto, Fra Angelico and Caravaggio (the *Taking of Christ* was discovered in the 1990s hanging on a wall in Leeson Street) all making an appearance. There are also works by Rembrandt and Vermeer from the Dutch school and a Spanish collection that includes Velázquez, El Greco and Picasso. The Irish collection is well worth checking out, with a wing dedicated to Jack Yeats.

ⓐ Merrion Square West and Clare St ⓣ 01 661 5133
ⓦ www.nationalgallery.ie ⓒ 09.30–17.30 Mon–Sat (till 20.30 Thurs), 12.00–17.30 Sun, closed bank holidays; admission charge for special exhibitions

National Museum of Archaeology and History

The building itself is worth the visit but once inside past the beautiful entrance hall, check out the hoards of gold unearthed from Irish bogs over the years, the exhibition on the 1916 Uprising, and the upper floors with Viking and medieval exhibits.

ⓐ Kildare St ⓣ 01 677 7444 ⓦ www.museum.ie ⓒ 10.00–17.00 Tues–Sat, 14.00–17.00 Sun, closed public holidays ⓑ Bus: 7, 7A, 8 (from Burgh Quay), 10, 11, 13 (from O'Connell St); DART: Pearse St

National Museum of Natural History

This little museum could have been created only by the Victorians. Founded in 1857, it is full of dried, pickled, pinned and stuffed things. Highlights include two giant elk skeletons which are 10,000 years old.

ⓐ Merrion St Upper ⓣ 01 677 7444 ⓦ www.museum.ie
ⓒ 10.00–17.00 Tues–Sat, 14.00–17.00 Sun ⓑ Bus: 7, 7A, 8 (from Burgh Quay); DART: Pearse St

THE CITY

RETAIL THERAPY

Grafton Street is a little enclave of British chain stores. Marks & Spencer is here, as are Gap, Max Mara, Benetton, Top Shop and Body Shop, but in between are some home-grown department stores, and the St Stephen's Green Shopping Centre has some interesting shops in its upper floors. Around Kildare Street are the real treasures of Irish shopping; just about every small art and crafts centre in Ireland is represented around here. Between Grafton Street and South Great George Street are lots of little classy clothes shops, antiques shops and more. Vintage clothes fans will enjoy a trek along South Great George Street, Aungier Street and Camden Street for the multitude of charity shops (and a few places which actually call themselves vintage clothes shops and charge more for the service). The following shops are worth seeking out:

A Wear Young clothes, lots of Irish designers at affordable prices. 26 Grafton St 01 671 7200 09.00–18.00 Mon–Wed, Fri & Sat, 09.00–20.00 Thur, 13.00–18.00 Sun

Brown Thomas Old-school, posh department store. Go to look and admire. Lots of designer outlets. 88–92 Grafton St 01 605 6666 09.00 18.00 Mon–Wed, Fri & Sat, 09.00–20.00 Thur, 12.00–18.00 Sun

BT2 Brown Thomas for the young. 28–29 Grafton St 01 605 6707 09.00–18.00 Mon–Wed, Fri & Sat, 10.00–20.00 Thur, 12.00–18.00 Sun

---

Have a rummage through a bookshop

THE IRISH TIMES

We look at life.
You live it.

THE CITY

Camden Street Market Fruit and veg, flowers and cheap clothes.
ⓐ 09.00–17.00 Mon–Sat

George's Street Arcade Covered market full of vintage clothes, books, CDs and inexpensive jewellery. Good café. ⓛ 09.00–19.00

The Kilkenny Store Lovely, lovely things on two floors from little craft shops all over the country, plus a great café. ⓐ 6 Nassau St
ⓣ 01 677 7066 ⓦ www.kilkennygroup.com

Magill's Delicatessen All you need for a picnic lunch. ⓐ 14 Clarendon St ⓣ 01 671 3830 ⓛ 09.00–17.00 Mon–Sat

Powerscourt Centre Classy shopping centre with not a chain store in sight. Lots of antiques, designer clothes, jewellery, kooky t-shirts and more. ⓐ 59 South William St ⓣ 01 679 4144 ⓛ 09.00–18.00 Mon–Wed, Fri & Sat, 09.00–20.00 Thur, 12.00–18.00 Sun

Rhinestones Possibly the nicest shop in Dublin. Antique jewellery of all kinds from the real thing to 1940s funky junk. ⓐ 18 Andrew St
ⓣ 01 679 0759 ⓛ 09.30–18.00 Mon–Wed, Fri & Sat, 09.30–20.00 Thur

Sheridan's Cheesemonger Lots of interesting cheeses from Ireland and abroad. ⓐ 11 South Anne St ⓣ 01 679 3143 ⓛ 09.00–17.00 Mon–Sat

Wild Child Vintage clothes in a street full of charity shops. ⓐ 61 South Great George St ⓣ 01 475 5099 ⓛ 10.00–18.00 Mon–Wed, Fri & Sat, 09.00–19.00 Thur

GRAFTON STREET & SURROUNDING AREA

TAKING A BREAK

Bewley's Café Bar £ ❶ For 160 years this place served tea and crumpets and fry-ups to the populace of Dublin, but in 2005 amidst great sighs and wailings it closed its doors only to reopen in the guise of a café bar. It's seriously affordable, family-orientated and offers modern cuisine with pizzas and pastas and innovative salads. While you're there check out the stained-glass windows by Harry Clark. ⓐ Bewley's Building, Grafton St ⓣ 01 672 7720 ⓦ www.cafebardeli.ie ⓛ 12.00–22.00 Sun–Wed, 12.00–23.00 Thur–Sat

Butlers Chocolate Café £ ❷ The best hot chocolate in town. ⓐ 51a Grafton St ⓣ 01 671 0599 ⓦ www.butlerschocolates.com

Café Bar Deli £ ❸ Another old Bewleys shop turned trendy. That's the way of the world. Nice food, pleasant surroundings, come back at night for the music. ⓐ 12–13 South Great George St ⓣ 01 677 1646 ⓛ 12.30–23.00 Mon–Sat, 14.00–22.00 Sun

Café en Seine £ ❹ Seriously over-the-top designer bar set in art deco France. Very affordable modern food. Jazz or traditional music on Sunday afternoons 15.00–17.00, and jazz band on Monday nights 22.00–24.00. ⓐ 39–40 Dawson St ⓣ 01 677 4567 ⓦ www.cafeenseine.com ⓛ 11.00–03.00

Juice £ ❺ This is as good as it gets for vegetarians in this city. Macrobiotic restaurant. Inexpensive lunches and funny-sounding drinks. Veggies should come back for dinner when there is an early bird menu and good à la carte options. ⓐ 73 South Great George St

① 01 475 7856 ② 12.00–22.00 Mon–Wed, 12.00–23.00 Thur & Fri, 10.00–23.00 Sat, 10.00–22.00 Sun

AFTER DARK

If you enjoy pub crawls you might like to check out the **Dublin Literary Pub Crawl**, which starts out in The Duke (Duke Street) and, along with some actors and storytellers, wanders the more literary pubs of the city. Nightly 19.30. Book in advance (① 01 670 5602 ⓦ www.dublinpubcrawl.com). Alternatively you can manufacture your own, less literary one by starting at the top of South Great George Street and working your way down.

Restaurants
One Pico £££ ❻ Service is excellent but then you are paying for it in this well-run, spacious, modern dining room. If you enjoy modern cooking at its best, make this the place you splash out on during your visit. ⓐ Molesworth Place ① 01 676 0300 ② 12.30–14.30 & 19.30–22.30 Mon–Sat, 19.30–22.00 Sun

Pearl Brasserie £££ ❼ Upmarket basement restaurant serving original, thoughtful French/Irish cuisine; foi gras and shellfish feature strongly. Lots of pillars give a sense of privacy. There's a nice bar area to settle in before eating, and good service. ⓐ 20 Merrion St Upper ① 01 661 3572 ② 12.30–14.30 & 17.30–22.30 Mon–Sat

Rubicon £££ ❽ Laid out over two floors, this place seems smaller and more intimate than it really is. Very modern, intelligent food with lots of Irish ingredients. Muted colours, log fires in winter. A bit overpowering for lunch, filled with people whose faces you feel you

GRAFTON STREET & SURROUNDING AREA

ought to recognise. ⓐ 6 Merrion Row ⓣ 01 676 1999 ⓞ 12.30–14.30 & 17.30–22.30 Mon–Sat, dinner only on Sun

Pubs & clubs
The Bailey Famous pub where Brendan Behan used to drink. By day it fills with shoppers and workers and has a huge lunch menu. By night it chills out a little and intellectuals get their nicotine fixes at the pavement tables. ⓐ 2 Duke St ⓣ 01 670 4939 ⓞ 11.30–23.30 (till 00.30 Sat)

▲ Bewley's, a great little day or night-spot

THE CITY

Carnival Cool dark interior on two levels. Very popular bar with a party atmosphere and no cover charge. ⓐ 11 Wexford St
ⓣ 01 405 3604

Davy Byrne's The famous pub that Leopold Bloom calls into in *Ulysses*. Always crowded with tourists and city folk. ⓐ 21 Duke St
ⓣ 01 677 5217 ⓞ 11.30–23.30 (till 00.30 Sat)

Gaiety Theatre This is actually a theatre but on Friday and Saturday nights, if there is no opera or ballet on, the place turns into a live music venue with salsa, jazz or soul. Attracts an older crowd.
ⓐ South King St ⓣ 01 677 1717

The Globe Quieter place in the maelstrom of partying, so a good place to start your pub crawl. Good food during the day too.
ⓐ 11 South Great George St ⓣ 01 671 1220 ⓞ 12.00–03.00 Mon–Sat, 12.00–23.00 Sun

Hogan's Two levels; the ground floor is, during the day, a pleasant café bar with huge windows open to the street where you can watch life passing by, and the basement opens late and rocks.
ⓐ 35 South Great George St ⓣ 01 677 5904 ⓞ 12.30–23.30 Mon–Wed, 12.30–00.30 Thur, 10.30–02.30 Fri & Sat, 15.00–23.00 Sun

The International Nice old pub full of character, with a club upstairs. Live jazz, blues or folk most nights, or comedy. ⓐ 23 Wicklow St
ⓣ 01 677 9250 ⓞ 11.30–23.30 (till 00.30 Sat)

J J Smyth's Basic pub, occasional live jazz and blues.
ⓐ 12 Aungier St

GRAFTON STREET & SURROUNDING AREA

Lillie's Bordello Still going strong after all these years. Fussy doormen though. Dress up for this place; A-listers will be here. ⓐ Grafton St ⓣ 01 679 9204 ⓦ www.lilliesbordello.ie

Lobby Bar/POD/Red Box/Craw Daddy The coolest places to be in Dublin after midnight. Who cares about celebrities when everyone looks so good? Four clubs all in one building. The Redbox is for throwing yourself around, POD for live acts, Craw Daddy and the Lobby Bar for looking serene. ⓐ Old Harcourt St Station, Harcourt St ⓣ 01 478 0166 ⓦ www.pod.ie

Long Hall Long, beautiful, old Victorian pub, no gimmicks or modish design features; just as it was a hundred years ago. ⓐ 51 South Great George St ⓣ 01 475 1590 ⓛ 16.00–23.30 Mon–Wed, 13.00–23.00 Thur, 13.00–00.30 Fri & Sat, 16.00–23.00 Sun

O'Donoghues One of the best places to go for impromptu traditional Irish sessions, but it can get very crowded with locals and tourists. ⓐ 15 Merrion Row ⓣ 01 660 7194 ⓦ www.odonoghues.ie ⓛ 10.30–23.30 Mon–Wed, 10.30–00.30 Thur–Sat, 12.30–23.00 Sun

The Sugar Club Very sophisticated place built in an old sugar factory. Live music most nights and occasional comedy nights. Lots of different bars to enjoy in one place. ⓐ Lower Leeson St ⓣ 01 678 7188 ⓦ www.thesugarclub.com

Whelan's Live music every night in this long-established bar. ⓐ 25 Wexford St ⓣ 01 478 0766

THE CITY

Temple Bar & surrounding area

Twenty years ago this area, between the river and Dame Street and from Fishamble Street to Fleet Street, was derelict, full of crazy little shops selling second-hand clothes, alternative music and the like, but as the Celtic Tiger cub grew to maturity, this place metamorphosed into the tourist-dedicated hot spot it is today. For all the blarney handed out, there is some genuine non-manufactured nightlife here (possibly a little too much on a Friday night when the hen parties are roaming) and good shops and places to visit. Around the perimeter of Temple Bar are some of the really big sights. After dark Temple Bar gives itself over entirely to fun. The pubs spill out onto the streets, the tourist shops open late, restaurants fill up and as the night wears on the clubs upstairs in the bars get going. At lunch-time every pub in the place has pub food, many have live music of some sort, and a considerable number have huge TV screens with some testosterone-driven activity showing. Check out www.templebar.ie for details of free concerts and performances in Temple Bar.

SIGHTS & ATTRACTIONS

City Hall
This handsome, 18th-century building was once the Royal Exchange. After 1801, when Dublin began its big decline, the building was no longer needed and it became an administrative centre. In the basement is an exhibition on the history of the city but it's worth popping in just for the stunning rotunda with its 5.5-m (18-ft) statue of Daniel O'Connell.

ⓐ Dame St ⓘ 01 222 2204 ⓦ www.dublincity.ie ⓛ 10.00–17.15

THE CITY

Mon–Sat, 14.00–17.00 Sun & bank holidays; admission charge
Bus: 77, 77A, 56A, 49 (from Eden Quay), 123 (from O'Connell St)

Meeting House Square
Not quite a Mediterranean piazza, but it's getting there. The square is home to a Sunday morning farmers' market where you can buy lumpy carrots and organic honey as well as some more esoteric stuff. In summer the square doubles as an open-air cinema and when it's warm enough the cafés that surround the square put out tables.

CULTURE

Chester Beatty Library
Chester Beatty was a seriously rich American with a tenuous link to Ireland who left his enormous collection of ancient manuscripts to the Irish state. For years it festered out in the sticks, but in 2000 it was brought into the city in all its glory. Well worth a visit.
Dublin Castle, Dame St 01 407 0750 10.00–17.00 Mon–Fri, 11.00–17.00 Sat, 13.00–17.00 Sun, closed Mon in winter; free admission

Christ Church Cathedral
Bits of this ancient building were erected in the 11th century when Dublin was a Viking city. Most of what you see is a Victorian makeover, including the tomb of Strongbow (the Norman conqueror of Ireland), but the place has a quality of its own. There is a museum of gold and silver bits and pieces in the crypt, and the floor tiles, replicas of the damaged medieval originals, are beautiful.
Christchurch Place 01 679 8991 www.cccdub.ie
09.00–18.00 (June–Aug); 09.45–17.00 (Sept–May); admission charge for crypt Bus: 49, 50, 51B, 54A, 56A, 65, 77, 77A, 78A, 123;

TEMPLE BAR & SURROUNDING AREA

DART: Tara St, then Bus 90 ❶ coins needed for automatic entrance to crypt

Dublin Castle
The place where Dublin Castle now stands was once a strategic location where the river Poddle (now underground) met the Liffey and a fort has stood here since early Christian times. The building you see before you is a more modern construct, now used when Ireland chairs the EU for official meetings. A visit here involves a very entertaining tour; the guides take you around the various sumptuous rooms and corridors, with graphic stories of the history of each room, and end up in the undercroft where you can make out the remains of the original fortifications.
ⓐ Dame St ❶ 01 645 8813 ⓦ www.dublincastle.ie ⓛ 10.00–16.45 Mon–Fri, 14.00–16.45 Sat, Sun & public holidays, closed 25 & 26 Dec, Jan 1 & Good Friday; admission charge ⓝ Bus: 77, 77A, 56A, 49 (from Eden Quay), 123 (from O'Connell St)

Dublinia & the Viking World
For a completely manufactured tourist destination, this is definitely one of the best. Set inside the old Synod Hall and linked to Christchurch Cathedral via an overhead bridge, the exhibition re-creates the sights, sound and smells of medieval and Viking Dublin. At the end of the exhibition you can climb to the top of St Michael's tower for stunning views over the city.
ⓐ St Michael's Hill ❶ 01 679 4611 ⓦ www.dublinia.ie ⓛ 10.00–17.00 (Apr–Sept); 11.00–16.00 Mon–Sat, 10.00–16.00 Sun & bank holidays (Oct–Mar); closed 23–26 Dec & 17 Mar; admission charge ⓝ Bus: 50 (from Eden Quay), 78A (from Aston Quay); Luas: Red Line (from Four Courts)

THE CITY

Gallery of Photography
The gallery has a permanent collection of 20th-century Irish photographs plus some excellent changing exhibitions.
ⓐ Meeting House Square ⓣ 01 671 4654
ⓦ www.irish-photography.com ⓞ 11.00–18.00 Tues–Sat, 13.00–18.00 Sun; free admission

National Photographic Archive
The National Library's collection of 600,000 photographs contains both historical and contemporary photographs, with subjects ranging from the political to the topographic.

🔺 *The Statue of Justice keeps watch over the city*

TEMPLE BAR & SURROUNDING AREA

⊙ Meeting House Square ⊙ 01 603 0200 ⊙ www.nli.ie
⊙ 10.00–17.00 Mon–Fri; free admission

RETAIL THERAPY

Once a bohemian, counter-culture ghetto, Temple Bar is now the place to go for a variety of gorgeous, if expensive, items, as well as some trashy get-it-for-the-in-laws stuff.

2Cool Design Mostly Scandinavian furniture but also some pretty design-conscious accessories, bits and pieces, rugs and textiles. ⊙ 4 Saul's Court, Cow's Lane ⊙ 01 672 5402 ⊙ www.2cooldesign.ie ⊙ 09.30–18.00 Mon–Fri, 10.00–17.30 Sat

Amnesty International Shop Books, Fair-Trade products, nice coffee bar and internet connection. ⊙ 48 Fleet St ⊙ 01 677 6361 ⊙ www.amnesty.ie ⊙ 09.00–17.30 Mon–Sat

Anthology Books Small bookshop in Meeting House Square. Definitely worth a browse. ⊙ Meeting House Square ⊙ 01 635 1422 ⊙ www.anthologystore.com ⊙ 09.30–17.30 Mon–Sat

The House of Astrology Tarot cards, aromatherapy oils, tumblestones, relaxation CDs, hypnosis tapes, books on astrology, tarot, alternative healing and more. ⊙ 9 Parliament St ⊙ 01 679 3404 ⊙ www.houseofastrology.com ⊙ 10.00–18.00 Mon–Sat

Irish Celtic Craftshop Not as naff as it sounds, this place has some good Irish designs in jewellery. ⊙ 10–12 Lord Edward St ⊙ 01 679 9912 ⊙ www.celticirishcrafts.com ⊙ 10.00–18.00 Mon–Sat

THE CITY

Meeting House Square Organic farmers' market. ● 08.00–14.00 Sat

Temple Bar Fashion Market Unique, one-off garments from some prestigious up-and-coming young Dubliners, children's wear, avant-garde and interesting objects, elegant handbags, purses and original accessories, hand-made and Italian resin jewellery and hand-blocked t-shirts. ⓐ Cow's Lane ● 10.00–17.30 Sat, 10.00–18.00 Christmas season (12, 19, 23 & 24 Dec), closed Jan

Temple Bar Jewellers Some pretty pieces of jewellery in traditional and modern designs. ⓐ 27 Eustace St ● 01 677 3647 ⓦ www.glycine.ie ● 09.00–17.30 Mon–Sat

Temple Wear Small, trendy clothes shop. ⓐ 3 Fownes St Upper ● 01 671 5253 ● 09.30–17.30 Mon–Sat

Whichcraft Cute craft items from around the world. Some excellent pieces of design. ⓐ Cow's Lane ● 01 670 9371 ⓦ www.whichcraft.com ● 09.00–18.00 Mon–Sat

TAKING A BREAK

The Bakery £ ❶ Lovely cakes, filled rolls and pastries to take out for a picnic or eat in with a coffee. ⓐ 8 Pudding Row, Essex St West ● 01 672 9882 ● 07.00–18.00 Mon–Fri, 07.00–17.00 Sat

Gallagher's Boxty House £ ❷ The place to try out this traditional Irish dish – potato pancakes filled with all manner of good things. ⓐ 20–21 Temple Bar ● 01 677 2762 ● 10.00–23.00 Mon–Fri, 10.00–23.00 Sat, 11.00–22.00 Sun

TEMPLE BAR & SURROUNDING AREA

Gruel £ ❸ Very popular, inexpensive, bare place serving soup and rolls as well as more substantial dishes. Good for lunch or an early evening eat-and-go kind of meal. ⓐ 68a Dame St ⓣ 01 670 7119 ⓒ 11.30–22.00 Mon–Sat, 11.30–21.00 Sun

Luigi Malone's £ ❹ Vast menu in a huge dining room with everything from pizzas to fajitas, ribs, burgers, fish and chips. Very popular at lunch-time, with children's menus and good lunch specials till 17.00. ⓐ Fownes St Lower ⓣ 01 679 2723 ⓒ 11.30–23.00

Eden ££ ❺ A great place for an evening meal but just as good for an afternoon coffee or lunch. Modern Irish cuisine in a stylish steel and beech dining room. ⓐ Meeting House Square ⓣ 01 670 5372 ⓒ 12.30–15.00 & 18.00–22.30 Mon–Fri, 19.00–23.00 Sat

Eliza Blue's ££ ❻ Some good lunch specials in this modern place with floor-to-ceiling windows overlooking the river. Good seafood options and vegetarians can also do well here. Good for dinner too. ⓐ 23 Wellington Quay ⓣ 01 671 9114 ⓒ 07.30–15.00 & 17.00–23.00 Mon–Fri, 08.00–16.00 & 17.00–23.00 Sat & Sun

Fitzer's ££ ❼ The enormous menu ranges around ciabatta, filled rolls, burgers and more modern European cuisine. Lots of tables outside. ⓐ Temple Bar Square ⓣ 01 679 0440 ⓒ 12.00–23.30

AFTER DARK

Restaurants
Monty's of Kathmandu £ ❽ One menu all day long so dinner doesn't suddenly become pricier than lunch. Lovely authentic

THE CITY

Nepalese food, cooked in one of the most long-standing and well-established restaurants. Monty's was here before Temple Bar became cool. Try their own label beer. ⓐ 28 Eustace St ⓣ 01 670 4911 ⓛ 12.00–14.30, 18.00–23.30 Mon–Sat, 11.00–23.30 Sun

FXB ££ ❾ Seriously meat-centred menu with free-range animals dished up by weight. Fish and vegetarian options too. Good early-bird menu. ⓐ 2 Crow St ⓣ 01 671 1248 ⓦ www.fxbrestaurants.com ⓛ 12.30–15.00 & 17.30–23.00

Nico's ££ ❿ Long-established Italian restaurant. White tablecloths, bus waiters but – thankfully – no Chianti bottles. ⓐ 53 Dame St ⓣ 01 677 3062 ⓛ 12.30–15.00 & 18.30–23.00 Mon–Sat, 12.00–15.30 & 18.00–21.00 Sun

Oliver St John Gogarty's ££ ⓫ Pure blarney, but isn't that what you came here for? Irish stew, huge bowls of mussels, copper things hanging on the walls and fiddly diddly music piped up from the bar downstairs. A bit cramped but bursting to the seams with satisfied customers. Reservations recommended, particularly at weekends. ⓐ 58–59 Fleet St ⓣ 01 671 1822 ⓛ 12.00–23.00 Mon–Sat, 16.00–23.00 Sun

Mermaid Café £££ ⓬ Nouvelle American cuisine in this popular place with very reasonable prices given the quality of the food. ⓐ 69–70 Dame St ⓣ 01 670 8236 ⓦ www.mermaid.ie ⓛ 12.30–15.00 & 18.30–23.00 Mon–Sat, 12.00–15.30 & 18.00–21.00 Sun

The Tea Room £££ ⓭ If you can't afford to stay at the Clarence you should eat here. The Tea Room offers excellent modern Irish cooking

TEMPLE BAR & SURROUNDING AREA

in an almost austere but elegant, refectory-style dining room. Very popular Sunday brunch. ⓐ Clarence Hotel, 6–8 Wellington Quay ⓣ 01 670 7766 ⓦ www.theclarence.ie ⓘ 12.30–15.00 & 18.30–23.00

Pubs & clubs

Club M Seriously dedicated nightclub with mirror balls and everything. DJs six nights a week. ⓐ Cope St ⓣ 01 671 5622 ⓦ www.clubm.ie ⓘ 20.00–02.00 Mon–Sat

▲ *Enjoy a good meal at the Clarence Hotel Tea Room*

THE CITY

Fitzsimons Everything you ever dreamed would be in a pub – DJs, food, upstairs club, big-screen telly. ⓐ Temple Bar
ⓦ www.fitzsimonshotel.com

Front Lounge Wine bar where all the really cool people hang out. Occasional live music and comedy nights. ⓐ 33–34 Parliament St
ⓣ 01 670 412 ⓛ 12.00–23.00 Mon–Wed & Sun, 12.00–01.30 Thur–Sat

Ha'penny Bridge Named after the bridge that it looks out on, this pub is best known for its open mike comedy night. ⓐ 42 Wellington Quay ⓦ www.battleoftheaxe.ie

Octagon The bar where the young and idealistic Bono sat and dreamed his dreams over a Guinness or two is now ultra sleek and a good place for cocktails. ⓐ 6–8 Wellington Quay ⓣ 01 407 0800
ⓦ www.theclarence.ie ⓛ 10.00–23.00 Mon–Sat, 12.30–22.30 Sun

Palace Where locals go for a quiet drink. ⓐ Fleet St

Temple Bar Music Centre Live music venue with a variety of activities on different nights from salsa classes to jazz or big-name bands in the 650-capacity dedicated club. ⓐ Curved St ⓣ 01 670 9202 ⓦ www.tbmc.ie

Turk's Head Good place for a knees up. Very tourist-oriented, garish bar, occasional live music. ⓐ 27–30 Parliament St ⓣ 01 679 9701
ⓛ 16.30–02.00

Viperoom Live lounge music seven nights in the bar and DJs doing their thing in the club upstairs. ⓐ 5 Aston Quay ⓣ 01 672 5566 ⓦ www.viperoom.ie

Theatres & cinemas

The Ark Children's theatre workshop which has regular programmes. ⓐ 11a Eustace St ⓣ 01 670 7788 ⓦ www.ark.ie

Crypt Arts Centre Small venue in the crypt of the Chapel Royal in Dublin Castle used by some of the more avant-garde theatre groups in the city. ⓐ Dublin Castle, Dame Street ⓣ 01 671 3387 ⓦ www.cryptartscentre.org

Irish Film Institute Independent foreign and low-budget Irish movies. ⓐ 6 Eustace St ⓣ 01 679 5744 ⓦ www.irishfilm.ie ⓒ booking from 13.30 daily

Olympia Theatre Dublin's surviving music hall where an enormous variety of productions take place. Worth checking out for the atmosphere. ⓐ 72 Dame St ⓣ 01 677 7744 ⓦ www.gaietytheatre.com

Project Arts Centre Two theatre spaces and a studio offer the city's most experimental theatre, art exhibitions, dance, regular live music, video and film. Also a nice bar. ⓐ 39 East Essex St ⓣ 01 679 6622 ⓦ www.project.ie

THE CITY

O'Connell Street & surrounding area

For many years, this was the downmarket part of the city where, even while the Celtic Tiger roared, buildings stood derelict and pound shops ruled. The area has seen great transformations in the last few years, with the Monument of Light replacing some pretty rubbishy statuary and the derelict quays turning into bijou housing for the upwardly mobile. The now well-established IFSC (International Financial Services Centre) is here with a few good places to eat, some shops, but a chiefly residential and business tone. At the very western extreme is The Point where many people will get their first experience of the city at a concert. North of O'Connell Street is some good, inexpensive accommodation and O'Connell Street itself is a historic part of the city where the major battle of the 1916 Uprising was waged; the bullet scars are still evident. In February 2006 new battles took place here when a basically Unionist march attempted to pass in front of the GPO (General Post Office) to commemorate the Protestants killed by the Republican paramilitaries over the decades.

SIGHTS & ATTRACTIONS

Boardwalk

Part of the effort to bring the north area of Dublin into the economic boom enjoyed by the rest of the city is the Boardwalk, which provides a pedestrian walkway along the north shore of the river where once only traffic heaved and blared. It is quite a pleasant walk, with benches for contemplating the nature of life in the city, and creates a link with Temple Bar across the road. It's a good place for a picnic lunch.

THE CITY

Custom House Visitor Centre

This is the place where in the old days ships had to park and declare what they were carrying and pay customs duties. When it was built in the 18th century, the merchants around Temple Bar tried to blow it up since its construction meant that their business, further up the river, would disappear. In 1921 the building was caught up in the civil war and was badly damaged. For many years an administrative centre, the place has recently had a facelift and contains an exhibition of the colourful history of the building and the city it serves.

ⓐ Custom House Quay ⓣ 01 888 2538 ⓛ 10.00–12.30 Mon–Fri, 14.00–17.00 Sat, Sun & bank holidays, closed Mon & Tues in winter; admission charge ⓝ DART: Tara St

O'Connell Street

Currently a bit of a building site while the new road layout is put in place, this street is a historical sight in itself. Until 1966, when the IRA blew it up, a giant statue of Lord Nelson stood here. It was followed by an ugly water feature called *Anna Livia* (the spirit of the Liffey), which has been retired to a warehouse and replaced by the *Monument of Light*, or whatever they're calling it this year (locals call it the 'stiletto in the ghetto'), a 120-m (393-ft) illuminated pole that was supposed to be completed for the millennium but didn't make it in time. At the heart of the street is the GPO, which became the headquarters of the Easter Rising and which was gutted, as were most of the other buildings around it, by shells from a British gunboat moored in the Liffey. If you stand under the portico of the building and peer upwards, some of the bullet holes are still preserved there (you can also see bullet holes in the statue of Daniel O'Connell, after whom the street was named, at the head of the street). In between the barriers around the building site (the paving

O'CONNELL STREET & SURROUNDING AREA

stones became missiles in February 2006) are the city's indigenous department stores, while along Moore Street is an open-air market. In Cathedral Street is St Mary's Pro-Cathedral, built in 1825, well out of sight of the British rulers of the time.

Parnell Square & The Garden of Remembrance
As Dublin decayed during the first 80 years of the 20th century, many of its beautiful Georgian buildings became derelict, but this square, one of the first of a big building spree in the 18th century,

▲ *Rest those legs by the River Liffey*

THE CITY

remains intact. Central is the Garden of Remembrance (1966) where the statue *Children of Lir* commemorates those who died in the struggle for independence. Originally a pleasure garden where the gentry paid to stroll about, the income from it went into building the Rotunda Maternity Hospital, the first maternity hospital in Europe, which still functions today.

🔺 *Children of Lir: another symbol of Ireland's historical struggles*

O'CONNELL STREET & SURROUNDING AREA

CULTURE

Dublin City Gallery: The Hugh Lane

Once upon a time this grand building in the centre of the north side of Parnell Square was the most des res in Dublin, built for the Earl of Charlemont in 1762. It currently houses the city's collection of modern Irish and European art. Entrance is free and for that you get works by Corot, Monet, Degas, Manet and Burne Jones, as well as a sound collection of works by Irish painters such as Sarah Purser, Jack Yeats and the artist who worked in stained glass, Harry Clarke. The highlight of a visit to the gallery, though, is the (not so free) workshop of Francis Bacon which was relocated here from London, every last paintbrush and beer bottle faithfully replaced.

Charlemont House, Parnell Square 01 874 1903

> **HUGH WHO?**
> When the *Lusitania* was torpedoed off the coast of County Cork in 1915, it left a pretty puzzle behind for the two governments of Britain and Ireland. Hugh Lane, the nephew of the Irish nationalist Lady Gregory, was on board and his will left his art collection to the state, which technically in 1915 was Britain. When Irish independence came in 1921, a quarrel arose over which state exactly he had meant. A partial resolution came in 1960 when the two governments agreed to share the collection, swapping stuff occasionally, but in 1968 Britain claimed the lot. The dispute was settled, again, by breaking up the collection, with half remaining permanently the property of the Irish state. One has to wonder how they managed to decide who got what.

THE CITY

ⓦ www.hughlane.ie ⓒ 09.30–18.00 Tues–Thur, 09.30–17.00 Fri & Sat, 11.00–17.00 Sun; admission charge for Francis Bacon Studio
ⓝ Bus: 3, 10, 11, 13, 16, 19

Dublin Writer's Museum
Anyone who has studied English Literature in any depth will be all too aware that a sizeable number of the really big names in Eng Lit are actually Irish – Joyce, Beckett, Yeats, Shaw, Swift, Heaney, Sheridan, Wilde and Behan, to name some of the heavyweights. This museum pays homage to many of these great white males with rare first editions, bits of their stuff, photographs and more, all set in another of the beautiful Georgian townhouses in Parnell Square, a sight in itself.
ⓐ 18 Parnell Square ⓣ 01 872 2077 ⓦ www.visitdublin.com
ⓒ 10.00–17.00 Mon–Sat (till 18.00 June–Aug), 11.00–17.00 Sun & public holidays; admission charge ⓝ Bus: 10, 11, 11B, 13, 13A, 16, 16A, 19, 19A; DART: Connolly Station

The James Joyce Centre
A centre dedicated to the life and works of James Joyce (who left Dublin at an early age!). Here you can see the door to 7 Eccles Street, where Leopold Bloom never lived, lots of first editions (banned for most of the 20th century), photographs and more. For somewhere with no Joyce connections at all except that a dancing master mentioned in *Ulysses* once lived here, it's a fun place, full of enthusiasts, and a good base for daily walking tours of the city, including Leopold Bloom's route in *Ulysses* and an excellent tour of Prospect Cemetery where Joyce's father is buried. Nice café and bookshop.
ⓐ 35 North Great George's St ⓣ 01 878 8547 ⓦ www.jamesjoyce.ie
ⓒ 09.30–17.00 Mon–Sat; admission charge for the centre and for the tours ⓝ Bus: 3, 10, 11, 11A, 13, 16A, 19, 19A, 22, 22A

O'CONNELL STREET & SURROUNDING AREA

ⓘ check website for possible changes in opening times after summer 2006

RETAIL THERAPY

The streets around O'Connell Street form one of the shopping centres in the city. Three big indigenous department stores offer everything from electrical goods to hatpins, the ILAC is full of little shops to explore, the Jervis Centre has a couple of big British stores and the streets leading off O'Connell – Talbot Street, Moore Street and Capel Street – all have something to offer, from daft Irish dancing kit to fake designer socks and antimacassars.

Arnotts A department store of the old school, tacked together from assorted buildings and full of things that your granny would buy as

▲ *Clery's has a stately presence in the heart of Dublin*

THE CITY

well as some modern clothes and a good coffee shop. ⓐ 12 Henry St
ⓣ 01 872 1111 ⓦ www.arnotts.ie ⓛ 09.00–18.30 Mon–Wed, Fri & Sat
(later Thur), 12.00–18.00 Sun

Clery's Purpose-built department store with huge windows and
some stylish things inside, including some good craft items.
ⓐ 18–27 O'Connell St ⓣ 01 878 6000 ⓦ www.clerys.com
ⓛ 09.00–18.00 Mon–Wed, Fri & Sat (later Thur)

Dunnes The Irish answer to M&S, with respectable clothes and
fashionable housewares. ⓐ Henry St ⓣ 01 671 4629
ⓦ www.dunnesstores.ie

▲ *'Pound of cherries for a euro!'*

O'CONNELL STREET & SURROUNDING AREA

Easons Excellent bookstore and newsagent with an extensive selection of maps, walking books and local history. ⓐ 40 O'Connell St ⓣ 01 858 3800 ⓦ www.eason.ie ⓑ 08.30–18.45 Mon–Wed, Fri & Sat (later Thur), 12.45–17.45 Sun

Roches Perhaps the John Lewis to Clerys' Selfridges but with a special Irish chaos factor built in. Good housewares, some nice clothes. ⓐ 54 Henry St ⓣ 01 873 0044

Moore Street Market Fruit and veg, Christmas wrapping paper, cheap toys, t-shirts and the like, all in a strong Dublin accent. ⓑ daily

Walton's Irish musical instruments as well as CDs and books. ⓐ 2 North Great George St ⓣ 01 874 7805 ⓑ 09.00–18.00 Mon–Sat

TAKING A BREAK

North of the river falls a bit short in the taking-a-break stakes, but there are some good places to look out for if you need a getting-out-of-the-heaving-crowds-of-O'Connell-Street moment. Clerys, Arnotts and Easons all have good, calming cafés, as does the James Joyce Centre, the Writer's Museum and the Hugh Lane. If you're a tapas fan check out the bar of the Halō restaurant (see page 98) in the Morrison Hotel where they serve them all afternoon.

Beshoff £ ❶ Great no-nonsense fish and chip place.
ⓐ 6 O'Connell St

Café Royal £ ❷ Very popular, excellent-value carvery lunch. Nothing outrageous here but some good, old-fashioned hotel food.

THE CITY

Try the afternoon tea. ⓐ Royal Dublin Hotel, O'Connell St ⓣ 01 873 3666 ⓞ 12.30–14.30 Mon–Fri

Epicurean Food Hall £ ❸ If you don't mind the hubbub this place is a seriously small food court with some esoteric stalls serving cuisine from around the world at very reasonable prices. ⓐ Liffey St Lower ⓞ 11.30–18.30 Mon–Sat

Grand Central £ ❹ Nicely converted old bank building serving some good lunch options and good coffee. Come back in the evening for the bar scene. ⓐ 10–11 O'Connell St ⓣ 01 872 8658 ⓞ 11.00–23.30 Mon–Thur, 11.00–02.00 Fri & Sat, 12.30–23.00 Sun

Patrick Conway's £ ❺ Big open bar serving some good pub food all day until 20.00. ⓐ 70 Parnell St ⓣ 01 873 2687 ⓦ www.patrickconways.com

Pravda £ ❻ Another café bar that really comes into its own in the evenings but is good for a wrap or a melt during the day. ⓐ 35 Liffey St Lower ⓣ 01 874 0076 ⓞ 12.00–23.30 Mon–Thur, 11.00–02.00 Fri & Sat, 12.30–23.00 Sun

AFTER DARK

Restaurants
Alilang Korean Restaurant ££ ❼ The city's only Korean restaurant, suitably adapted to the less fiery Irish palate. Here you can eat *kimchee*, barbecue your own food at the table and try the green tea

◐ *One of Dublin's richly traditional pubs*

THE CITY

and Korean beer. ⓐ 102 Parnell St ⓣ 01 874 6766 ⓦ www.alilangkoreanrestaurant.com ⓒ 12.00–14.30 & 17.30–23.30 Mon–Thur, 12.00–14.30 & 17.30–00.30 Fri, midday–midnight Sat & Sun

D One Restaurant ££–£££ ❽ One of the most strangely located restaurants in the city, this small but cutting edge glass box stands right on the banks of the Liffey. The cuisine is thoughtful, modern Irish. Very busy at lunch-time but there is a good-value early dinner menu till 19.30. Outdoor tables in summer. ⓐ North Wall Quay ⓣ 01 856 1622 ⓒ 12.00–15.00 & 17.00–22.00 Mon–Sat, 12.00–17.00 Sun

Chapter One £££ ❾ One of the best restaurants in the city, this place has survived for many a year in the basement of the beautiful Georgian Writer's Museum. Excellent cooking, lots of organic food, and the theatre menu brings prices down to almost affordable. ⓐ 18–19 Parnell Square ⓣ 01 873 2266 ⓒ 12.30–14.30 & 18.00–23.00 Tues–Fri, 18.00–23.00 Sat

Halõ £££ ❿ Very stylish restaurant in the Morrison Hotel, and unusually for a hotel restaurant it serves excellent avant-garde food. Very young, wealthy clientele enjoy a seriously designed dining room. ⓐ Morrison Hotel, Ormond Quay Lower ⓣ 01 887 2420 ⓒ lunch 12.00–15.00, tapas 15.00–18.00, dinner 18.00–22.30 ⓘ reservations essential

Clubs

Murphy's Laughter Lounge Recently rebuilt at vast expense, this stand-up comedy venue has it all – comfortable auditorium, cameras carrying the performances to two bars via enormous plasma screens,

O'CONNELL STREET & SURROUNDING AREA

and some big names in comedy three nights a week. ⓐ 4–8 Eden Quay ⓣ 01 878 3003 ⓞ 19.30 Thur–Sat; admission charge

Spirit A variety of spiritual states, none of them particularly connected with loud music and alcohol, are the names given to the various areas of this vast entertainment centre with club, chill-out room, dance floors and performance area. Check the website for rates and what's on. ⓐ 57 Middle Abbey St ⓣ 01 877 9999 ⓦ www.spiritdublin.com ⓞ 22.00–03.00 Thur–Sat

▲ 'The Hags with the Bags' – no, seriously!

THE CITY

West of the city centre

The area west of the city centre is dominated by the enormous Phoenix Park, the biggest public park in Europe, and behind it the Prospect Cemetery whose tombstones read like a roll-call of the public personalities of the last 150 years. Along the north bank of the Liffey is the newly renovated north quays area, which leads to Smithfield and then on to the Collins Barracks and the park. On the south side of the river are the Guinness Storehouse, the Museum of Modern Art and Kilmainham Jail. A few other places are well worth seeking out a little way north and south of the river. It is while discovering this part of the city that you may find the Luas tram useful. There isn't much as yet in this area in the way of shops but one or two places are emerging.

SIGHTS & ATTRACTIONS

Chimney Viewing Tower

Once the chimney of the Jameson Distillery, this 56-m (185-ft) tower now has a lift, viewing platform and entrance charge. There are nice views from the top and at Christmas Santa lives up there.

ⓐ Chief O'Neill's Hotel, Smithfield ⓣ 01 817 3838 Ⓝ Bus: 25, 25A, 67, 67A (from Middle Abbey St), 68, 69, 79 (from Aston Quay), 90 (from Connolly, Tara & Heuston stations); Luas: Red Line to Smithfield

Dublin Zoo

A thoughtful zoo with its inmates as happy as such creatures can be. There is a train ride, wildlife shows, and several endangered species represented here.

ⓐ Phoenix Park ⓣ 01 474 8900 ⓦ www.dublinzoo.ie ⓛ 09.30–18.00

West of the city centre

WEST OF THE CITY CENTRE

Mon–Sat, 10.30–18.00 Sun (Mar–Sept); 09.30–dusk Mon–Sat, 10.30–dusk Sun (Oct–Feb); admission charge ◎ Bus: 10, 10A (from O'Connell St), 25, 25A, 26, 66, 66A, 66B, 67, 67A (from Middle Abbey St), 68, 69

Guinness Storehouse

Its lack of high buildings and position in a valley surrounded by mountains makes Dublin a grand spot for getting up high and checking out the view. Besides offering a tour of the history of one of the most famous breweries in the world, the Guinness Storehouse affords visitors the best opportunity for seeing the city from Gravity, the 360-degree viewing room at the top of the brewery.

ⓐ St James Gate ⓣ 01 408 4800 ⓦ www.guinness-storehouse.com ⓛ 09.30–17.00 (till 20.00 July & Aug), closed Christmas Day, St Stephen's Day & Good Friday ◎ Bus: 51B, 78A (from Aston Quay), 123 (from O'Connell St); Luas: Red Line to St James Hospital

Old Jameson Distillery

Another former glory of the city turned into a visitor centre. The Old Jameson Distillery visit is by tour around all the milling, mashing, fermenting tanks, ending up with a visit to the bar and a free whiskey-tasting session when the guide asks for a volunteer to taste several types of the tipple. Be ready!

ⓐ Bow St ⓣ 01 807 2355 ⓦ www.jamesondistillery.ie ⓛ 09.30–18.00 (last tour begins at 17.30), closed Christmas Day, St Stephen's Day & Good Friday; admission charge ◎ Bus: 68, 69, 79 (from Aston Quay), 90 (from Connolly & Heuston stations); Luas: Red Line to Smithfield

◐ *Prepare yourself for an interesting tour*

THE CITY

Phoenix Park
A whole day's visit in itself, this park is enormous, complete with its own herd of deer, a lacklustre visitor centre, a 17th-century tower house, a zoo, a police museum and lots of statuary. It is the home to the American ambassador and the Irish president, a war memorial garden designed by Lutyens and lots of people having a day out. Pick a sunny Saturday when there are free tours of Áras an Uachtaráin, the president's house.

❶ 01 677 0095 ❷ www.heritageireland.ie ❸ visitor centre 09.30–17.30 (later in summer); admission charge ❶ Phoenix Park, like most city parks, is not a particularly safe place to wander at night

CULTURE

Four Courts
This is Dublin culture at its most raw. The courts were built in the 18th century and still fulfil their original function. During court sittings you can go inside and watch criminals being found innocent or guilty. During the civil war these buildings were the site of a fierce battle between the two sides and, like the GPO, still bear the scars of battle.

❸ Inns Quay ❸ court sittings 11.00–13.00 & 14.30–17.00 Oct–July

Irish Jewish Museum
In the 19th century, Dublin had a thriving Jewish quarter centred around the Portobello area of the city, with several synagogues, Jewish bakeries, craft workshops and shops. The area is fast becoming a bijou suburb for regular Dubliners and all that remains of the old culture is this little museum, set in what was once a small local synagogue. The upstairs remains the synagogue while

WEST OF THE CITY CENTRE

downstairs a 19th-century Jewish kitchen is set out and there is an exhibition of memorabilia. This latter charts the Irish state's relationship with its resident Jewish community over the 20th century, which explains a lot about why Dublin (and Ireland) is having so much trouble accepting the new waves of European immigrants.

📍 3–4 Walworth St, off Victoria St ☎ 01 490 1857 🕐 11.00–15.30 Sun, Tues & Thur (May–Sept); 10.30–14.30 Sun (Oct–Apr) 🚌 Bus: 16, 16A, 19, 19A, 122 (to Victoria St), 14, 14A, 15, 15A, 15B, 15C, 15X, 65, 65B, 83 (to South Richmond St)

Irish Museum of Modern Art

The museum hosts an ever-changing series of exhibitions of modern art from the national collection and foreign artists' work, set in the beautiful old Royal Hospital, one of the city's oldest buildings. The complex includes artists' studios which you can occasionally peek into, a formal garden, and Bully's Acre, a medieval burial ground. There are occasional tours of the building showing some of the surviving panelling and interiors.

📍 Royal Hospital, Military Rd ☎ 01 612 9900 🌐 www.imma.ie
🕐 10.00–17.30 Tues–Sat, 12.00–17.30 Sun & bank holidays, closed Christmas Day, St Stephen's Day & Good Friday 🚌 Bus: 26 (from Wellington Quay), 51, 51B, 78, 79 (from Aston Quay), 90 (from Connolly & Tara stations), 123 (from O'Connell St)

Kilmainham Gaol

Opened in 1794 just in time to take in the rebels of the 1798 uprising and closing in 1924 after the last of the civil war prisoners were released, the gaol charts the history of the fight for Irish independence. The building was hated and stood derelict for

THE CITY

decades after it was closed, until a few enthusiasts got permission to begin renovating it. Now that the pain of those early years has begun to wear off, the gaol has become a tourist attraction. Leading figures in Irish history spent time here, as did thieves, murderers and other criminals. Executions were carried out in the yard and the bodies of rebels buried in quicklime so that they couldn't be re-interred later. The visit is by tour and is a fascinating insight into what prison life was like. A small museum tells the history of the prison and can be visited before the tour begins.

ⓐ Inchicore Rd, Kilmainham ⓣ 01 453 5984
ⓦ www.heritageireland.ie ⓛ 09.30–17.00 (Mar–Oct); 09.30–16.00 Mon–Sat, 10.00–17.00 Sun (Oct–Mar); admission charge ⓝ Bus: 51B, 51C, 78A, 79, 79A (from Aston Quay)

Marsh's Library

The oldest public library in Ireland was built on the instructions of Bishop Marsh in 1701. The interior is exactly as it was 305 years ago, with special cages around the most valuable books. In the visitors book you can see some famous names and in the Delmas Conservation Bindery you can watch old volumes being restored.

ⓐ St Patrick's Close ⓣ 01 454 3511 ⓦ www.marshlibrary.ie
ⓛ 10.00–13.00 & 14.00–17.00 Mon & Wed–Fri, 10.00–13.00 Sat; admission charge ⓝ Bus: 50, 54A, 56A (from Eden Quay)

National Museum of Decorative Arts & History at Collins Barracks

This is one of those excellent museums that, instead of concentrating on the preserved beautiful things that rich people used, is filled with rustic furniture, half-reconstructed carriages,

▶ *St Patrick: window by Heaton, Butler & Bayne (1890)*

387

THE CITY

everyday clothing, and more (as well, of course, as the regulation expensive pots and ornaments of the wealthy). One section, called the 'curators' choice', is a series of drawers which visitors can open to observe the bits that the curators like the most. There are videos on how to make straw baskets, courses for children, a nice coffee shop and a bookshop.

Benburb St 01 677 7444 www.museum.ie 10.00–17.00 Tues–Sat, 14.00–17.00 Sun Bus: 90 (from Aston Quay), 25, 25A, 66, 67 (from Middle Abbey St); Luas: Red Line to Museum

Prospect Cemetery

Not normally associated with tourist destinations, this cemetery is filled to the brim with the famous dead of Ireland. At the centre is the enormous round tower dedicated to Parnell, one of the country's major heroes. Here, too, is Michael Collins, buried close to his sweetheart Kitty Kiernan. Enormous marble tombs mark the dead of the Catholic hierarchy while more modest stones mark Gerard Manley Hopkins and Brendan Behan (the circular hole in his tombstone is often filled by his followers with a glass of Guinness). The rebels of 1916 are for the most part here, as is De Valera, the country's first president, whose grave is the most vandalised one in the cemetery. Buy a map in the flower shop and wander, or join one of the excellent and amusing free tours.

Finglas Rd, Glasnevin 01 830 1133 www.glasnevin-cemetery.ie dawn–dusk; tours 14.30 Wed & Fri, 11.30 Sun (May–Sept); tours Wed & Fri only (Oct–Apr)

St Michan's Church

Not yet turned into a heritage centre, this ancient church has much to offer visitors. It was founded in 1095 and was once the major

WEST OF THE CITY CENTRE

church in this part of the city. The current building dates back to 1686. Its chief draw, however, is not in its architecture but in the vaults where the bodies of those interred have remained undecayed for several centuries.

ⓐ Church St ⓣ 01 872 4154 ⓔ stmichans@iol.ie ⓛ 10.00–12.30 & 14.00–16.30 Mon–Fri, 14.00–16.30 Sat (Mar–Oct); 12.30–15.30 Mon–Fri, 10.00–12.45 Sat (Nov–Feb); admission charge Ⓝ Bus: 25, 25A, 26, 37, 51, 66, 66A, 68, 69, 134

St Patrick's Cathedral
Founded in 1191 this cathedral is built on a spot where St Patrick is said to have baptised the first Christians in Ireland. Much of the medieval interior of the church remains, although like Christ Church Cathedral, it had a 19th-century facelift. The tombs of Jonathan Swift and his companion Stella are here, as is an enormous monument to the Boyle family. As you enter the church, note the number of steps you have to go down to get in; the floor of the church was at street level in medieval times.

ⓐ Saint Patrick's Close ⓣ 01 475 4817 ⓦ www.stpatrickscathedral.ie ⓛ 09.00–18.00 Mon–Fri, 09.00–17.00 Sat, 09.00–15.00 Sun;

> **CHANCING YOUR ARM**
> In the north transept of St Patrick's Cathedral is a wooden door, said to be 15th century. The hole in the door was made when, after a fight between two warring lords, one barricaded himself behind it in what was then the chapter house. The other, braver, lord cut the hole and stuck his arm through in an effort to make peace, giving us the expression 'chancing your arm'.

THE CITY

admission charge ⓝ Bus: 54A, 56A (from Eden Quay) ⓘ during services admission is for worshippers only

Shaw's Birthplace

If you are fed up with Georgian Dublin then this is the place to visit, full of Victoriana and laid out just as a middle-class Victorian family would have lived. For a brief period, the family in question was that of George Bernard Shaw, although the Victorian theme is slightly more interesting than the literary one.

ⓐ 33 Synge St ⓣ 01 475 0854 ⓦ www.visitdublin.com ⓛ 10.00–13.00 & 14.00–17.00 Mon, Tues, Thur & Fri, 14.00–17.00 Sat, Sun & public holidays, closed Oct–Apr; admission charge ⓝ Bus: 16, 16A, 19, 19A, 122

RETAIL THERAPY

Out of the city centre, shops generally tend to be pretty functional places but there are a few streets worth a browse here. Francis Street contains a series of antique shops and markets dealing in bric-a-brac, furniture and memorabilia and is well worth seeking out. At Smithfield is Duck Lane, a tourist-dedicated place selling arts and crafts and housewares. The National Museum at Collins Barracks has a good bookshop, selling books on Irish history and some craft items, while at the Old Jameson Distillery there are whiskey-related things to buy.

TAKING A BREAK

1780 £ ❶ This public bar in the Old Jameson Distillery does a popular pub lunch. ⓐ Bow St, Smithfield ⓣ 01 807 2355 ⓛ lunch 12.00–14.30

WEST OF THE CITY CENTRE

The Brazen Head £ ❷ Better known for its nightly traditional music, this, the oldest pub in the city, also does a good carvery lunch and bar food throughout the afternoon till 21.00. Live music all Sunday afternoon. It also has an attractive restaurant upstairs serving modern Irish cuisine in an olde worlde atmosphere.
ⓐ 20 Bridge St ⓣ 01 677 9549 ⓦ www.brazenhead.com

O'Shea's Merchant £ ❸ Functional-looking bar that does a good bar lunch. ⓐ 12 Lower Bridge St ⓣ 01 679 3797 ⓛ lunch 12.00–18.00

▲ St Patrick's Cathedral choir was founded in 1432

THE CITY

The Park Café Bar £ ❹ This rather good extension of the lobby of the Park Inn does filled rolls, pannini, wraps and more substantial dishes. Outside seating in the pleasant square gets you away from the occasionally intense music. ⓐ Park Inn, Smithfield Village ❶ 01 817 3838 ⏰ lunch 12.00–14.30, sandwiches 15.00–17.00, evening menu 17.00–21.00

🔺 *Enjoy a drink or two at Cobblestone*

WEST OF THE CITY CENTRE

Nancy Hands ££–£££ ❺ Utterly inauthentic pub that looks as if it's been there since the Industrial Revolution. Carvery lunch, coffees and a pleasant place for dinner. ⓐ 30 Parkgate St ⓣ 01 677 0177 ⓛ 11.00–23.30 (later at weekends), lunch 12.00–14.00, dinner 19.30–21.00

AFTER DARK

Restaurants

Kelly & Ping ££ ❻ Asian fusion place serving an innovative mix of Irish and Asian dishes. Quite stunning black and red décor; good place to make a night of it before seeking out some late night live music. ⓐ Park Inn, Smithfield Village ⓣ 01 817 3840 ⓛ 12.00–late Mon–Fri, 17.00–late Sat

Ryan's ££ ❼ Upstairs in this Victorian pub is a restaurant serving Irish cuisine in Victorian-style surroundings (see page 114).

Bars & clubs

The Brazen Head Live traditional music every night (see page 111).

The Chancery Inn Quaint and curious old pub which opens at 07.00 every morning except Sunday, serving traders from the nearby Smithfield fruit and vegetable market. Colourful locals, and karaoke every Friday and Saturday night at 21.00. ⓐ 1 Inns Quay ⓣ 01 677 0420 ⓛ 07.00–23.30 Mon–Thur, 07.00–late Fri & Sat

Cobblestone Cracking old pub which survived the devastation of rebranding Smithfield as a tourist attraction. Live traditional music

THE CITY

downstairs and a pay-as-you-enter live venue upstairs. ⓐ King St North ⓣ 01 872 1799

Dice Bar Hip New York-style bar which has resisted the temptation to get themed. Occasional live music. Check listings for what's on. Nice cocktails. ⓐ 79 Queen St, Smithfield ⓣ 01 674 6710 ⓞ 12.30–23.30 (later at weekends)

The Legal Eagle Occasionally known as 'The Bar', this place has DJs most nights and the occasional live music session. ⓐ 1–2 Chancery Place, Four Courts ⓣ 01 873 5031 ⓞ 12.30–23.30 (later at weekends)

O'Shea's Merchant Set dancing most evenings upstairs after the food has been cleared away (see page 111).

Ryan's This place looks so good it has to be fake, but unlike Nancy Hands next door which is entirely built from architectural salvage, it's as real as they come. Lovely old bar fittings and a Victoriana restaurant upstairs. ⓐ 22 Parkgate St ⓣ 01 677 6097 ⓞ 12.30–23.30 (later at weekends)

Voodoo Lounge Laid-back, late-opening pub and live venue with dance area, pizza stand, and a nice garden in the summer. DJs and live bands throughout the week and because it's out of the way of the maelstrom of Temple Bar, it is rarely crowded. ⓐ 39–40 Arran Quay, Smithfield ⓣ 01 873 6013 ⓞ 12.00–23.00 (later at weekends)

▶ *The outstanding beauty of Howth*

OUT OF TOWN trips

OUT OF TOWN

The northern coastline & Newgrange

For decades wealthy Dubliners have been leaving the city and heading for the towns to the north, commuting in each day and creating a suburban feel in these small places. If you want to venture out of Dublin, a trip north starts at Howth, which retains a sleepy, fishing-village demeanour. Beyond Howth, Malahide has lots to offer with a lovely coastal walk, Malahide Castle and gardens. Further north again, Skerries has some pretty coastline and a seaside-haven feel and is well worth considering as a place to stay outside the city. The highlight of a trip north, and one which is best conducted through a tour agency, is the trip to Newgrange in the Boyne Valley, a 4,500-year-old, perfectly engineered underground series of passage tombs and burial chambers.

A railway line trundles its way north along the coast and all the seaside towns are easily accessed with the DART. For Newgrange there is a bus service from Busáras in Store Street directly to the Brú na Bóinne Visitor Centre, from where a shuttle bus takes you to the sites. The sights and attractions in this section are presented in the order that you would encounter them on a train trip north.

SIGHTS & ATTRACTIONS

Howth Village

Howth is a pretty seaside town. A couple of wacky museums are located here and there are some interesting places to eat, although you wouldn't travel out here just for the restaurants. The highlight of a day in Howth is the cliff walk around the Howth peninsula. Make your way across the grounds of Howth Castle to Carrickbrack Road where a sign indicates the start of the cliff walk. An alternative

OUT OF TOWN

is to start from Sutton Station where Station Road and then Greenfield Road will lead to the cliff walk. The paths are clearly marked and the walk takes about two hours, finishing in Balscadden Road in the village where there are lots of places to recuperate.

National Transport Museum
This is a bus and fire engine geek paradise with 60 or more commercial vehicles dating back to the earliest forms of motorised transport.
ⓐ Howth Castle Demesne ⓣ 01 848 0831
ⓦ www.nationaltransportmuseum.org ⓒ 10.00–17.00 Mon–Sat (June–Aug); 14.00–17.00 Sat, Sun & bank holidays (Sept–May); admission charge ⓝ Bus: 31, 31B (from Eden Quay); DART: Howth

Ye Olde Hurdy Gurdy Museum
Every bit as tacky as the name suggests. Old radios and TVs, Morse code equipment, gramophones, etc. Worth visiting for some as a trip down memory lane.
ⓐ Martello Tower, Abbey St, Howth ⓣ 086 815 4189 ⓦ www.qsl.net
ⓒ 11.00–17.00 daily (May–Oct); 11.00–16.00 Sat & Sun (Nov–Apr); admission charge ⓝ Bus: 31, 31B (from Eden Quay); DART: Howth

Malahide Village
This is serious dormitory town territory, somnolent during weekdays and buzzing with life at weekends. The village itself has one or two interesting restaurants but the main reason to come here is to visit Malahide Castle. From the village there is an excellent walk, mostly along paved seafront, to Portmarnock, where afternoon tea at the White Sands Hotel makes a pleasant break.
ⓝ Bus: 42 (from Dublin city centre); DART & suburban rail: Malahide

THE NORTHERN COASTLINE & NEWGRANGE

Fry Model Railway
One for small boys and anoraks, this collection was put together by Cyril Fry, a railway engineer.
ⓐ Malahide Castle Demesne ⓣ 01 846 3779 ⓦ www.visitdublin.com
ⓛ 10.00–13.00 & 14.00–17.00 Mon–Thur & Sat, 14.00–18.00 Sun & public holidays (Apr–Sept only); admission charge

Malahide Castle
Originally built in the 12th century and owned by the Talbot family for 800 years, this fortified house has been restored to its original condition and is open to the public by tour. It's a fascinating tour, omitting only the below-stairs section, and includes a peek into a haunted side room, and collections of silhouettes and model furniture. A considerable number of portraits on permanent loan from the National Gallery are also kept here. The castle grounds are extensive and include a little walled garden and the ruins of a 14th-century abbey.
ⓣ 01 846 2184 ⓦ www.malahidecastle.com ⓛ 10.00–17.00 Mon–Sat, 10.00–18.00 Sun & public holidays (Apr–Sept); 10.00–17.00 Mon–Sat, 11.00–17.00 Sun & public holidays (Oct–Mar); admission charge

Tara's Palace
Begun in 1980 and still in the process of completion, this is every Barbie owner's dream. Oil paintings adorn the palace walls, and the place is filled with crystal glassware, perfect miniature furniture, state and private rooms, plus Oscar Wilde's mother's dolls' house and lots of dolls and antique toys.
ⓐ The Courtyard, Malahide Castle Demesne ⓣ 01 846 3779
ⓛ 10.45–16.45 Mon–Fri, 11.30–17.30 Sat, Sun & public holidays

OUT OF TOWN

(Apr–Sept); 11.30–17.30 Sat, Sun & public holidays (Oct–Mar); admission charge

Newbridge House & Traditional Farm

This place is worth the effort of getting there, even with its slightly more problematic access. It's an 18th-century mansion once owned by the archbishop of Dublin. The rooms that are open to the public are furnished in the original style, but more interestingly, the house's original outbuildings are intact and have been brought back to their former condition, including the dairy that provided the bishop's milk and butter, one of his estate workers' cottages, a smithy and a workshop. In the extensive grounds is a traditional farm complete with the animals that the bishop's household would have kept.

ⓐ Newbridge Demesne, Donabate ⓣ 01 843 6534 ⓦ www.fingal-dublin.com ⓛ 10.00–13.00 & 14.00–17.00 Tues–Sat, 14.00–18.00 Sun & public holidays (Apr–Sept); 14.00–17.00 Sat, Sun & public holidays (Oct–Mar); admission charge ⓝ Suburban Rail: northbound from Connolly or Pearse St Station to Donabate, then a 15-minute walk; Bus: 33B from Eden Quay to Donabate

Skerries Village

Even dedicated commuters consider Skerries a bit too far out to commute from, and Skerries village makes an excellent base if you have time on your hands and no love for late city nights. Several houses here are still thatched and a small fishing fleet operates out of the harbour. There are some fine walks around Red Island, a sandy tombolo, and the walk along the foreshore can be extended while the tide is out as far as Rush, to the south of Skerries.

THE NORTHERN COASTLINE & NEWGRANGE

Skerries Mills

Not just a heritage centre, these are working mills, dating back to the 16th century and once owned by an Augustinian monastery. As water and wind power gave way to electricity, the mills fell into disuse, but the bakery operated right up until the 1980s. Now fully restored, the mills comprise two windmills and a water mill. You can watch the flour being ground and have a go yourself and then fill up with bread and cakes in the café. There's also a nice craft shop. The complex operates as the local tourist office too.

ⓐ Skerries ⓣ 01 849 5208 ⓦ www.skerriesmills.org ⓒ 10.30–17.30

▲ *Malahide Castle*

OUT OF TOWN

(Apr–Sept); 10.30–16.30 (Oct–Mar); closed Good Friday & two weeks over Christmas; admission charge ⓑ Bus: 33 from Eden Quay; Suburban Rail: Skerries

Ardgillan Castle

Built in 1738, this house was in private hands until 1982. It has been furnished in the style of the 19th century and its biggest attraction is the below-stairs part where the working conditions and utensils of the family servants are to be seen. In the upper storeys of the house there is an exhibition of the Down Survey, commissioned by Oliver Cromwell. The most spectacular part of the visit, though, is the grounds. The house is set on a hill and from the wooded gardens there are fine views all the way to the Mountains of Mourne. You can also visit a heated Victorian glasshouse, complete with lemon trees, and a walled garden. Somewhere in the grounds, too, is the ice house, used to keep perishable food cool in the summer.

ⓐ Balbriggan ⓘ 01 849 2212 ⓒ house 11.00–18.00 Tues–Sun & public holidays (Apr–Sept); 11.00–16.30 Tues–Sun & public holidays (Oct–Mar); park 10.00–dusk; guided tours of the gardens 15.30 Thur (June–Aug); admission charge ⓑ Bus: 33 from Eden Quay; Suburban Rail: Skerries, then a 30-minute walk

Newgrange & Knowth

Discovered in 1699, this Neolithic passage grave consists of a 19-m (62-ft) sloping passage leading to a central chamber with a corbelled roof. Set into this is a light box which allows sunlight into the room for about 17 minutes around the winter solstice. Don't even think about going there for that experience, as places for a visit are booked for decades to come, but the operators have fitted up a fake sunlight so you can imagine what it must be like. The interior is

THE NORTHERN COASTLINE & NEWGRANGE

decorated with carved lozenge and zig-zag patterns and a massive stone covered the entrance, presumably to be pulled aside each year at the winter solstice. In summer people come here in droves and there is often a long wait for access.

Close to Newgrange and rather less well known is a whole series of Knowth passage tombs, the largest being two of these tombs built back to back. The eastern passage is an enormous 40 m (130 ft) long, and its chamber is built in the shape of a cross. Sadly, though, while the interior has many more decorated stones than Newgrange, it is not possible to enter the graves. The bus tours from

● *An aerial view of Newgrange Megalithic Passage Tomb*

OUT OF TOWN

the visitor centre can be taken to either or both Neolithic sites.
ⓐ Brú na Bóinne Visitre Centre, Domore ⓣ 041 982 0300
ⓦ www.knowth.com ⓛ 09.00–19.00 (June–mid-Sept); 09.00–18.00
(May & end Sept); 09.30–17.30 (Mar–Apr & Oct); 09.30–17.00
(Nov–Feb); admission charge ⓝ Bus: from Busáras, Store St, to Domore

RETAIL THERAPY

Malahide is about the best you will find if you are desperate to do some shopping north of Dublin city centre. It is small enough to get to know all the shops in about 20 minutes – a couple of bookshops, some sophisticated dress shops, and a couple of charity shops where the wealthy of Malahide take their cast-offs.

TAKING A BREAK

Howth
Caffè Caira £ Seriously popular fish and chip shop with a few seats inside but most people sit out on the harbour wall. No newspaper wrappers, but almost the real thing. ⓐ 1 East Pier ⓛ 12.30–21.00

The Bloody Stream ££ Café bar beside the station with a substantial lunch menu weekdays from 12.00 to 20.00 (till 18.30 weekends). The restaurant upstairs operates at weekends. Standard, well-cooked fare of steaks and salads, wraps and filled rolls. ⓐ Howth Railway Station ⓣ 01 839 5076

Malahide
Lounge Bar, White Sands Hotel £ If you've done the bracing seaside walk from Malahide, this is a great place to stop for a break. Coffee

THE NORTHERN COASTLINE & NEWGRANGE

at the bar or lunch is available seven days a week. ⓐ White Sands Hotel, Coast Rd, Portmarnock ⓣ 01 846 0420 ⓛ 12.30–15.00 Mon–Sat, 12.30–18.00 Sun

Cruzzo Restaurant ££–£££ Trendy place doing modern Irish cuisine, coffees and a clubby atmosphere at night. ⓐ The Marina, Malahide ⓣ 01 845 0599 ⓦ www.cruzzo.ie ⓛ 12.30–14.30 & 18.00–22.15 Tues–Sat, 12.30–15.00 & 18.00–22.00 Sun; early bird menu 18.00–19.00

Skerries
Parachute Café £ Coffee shop in the village with a children's play area and seating outside. Breakfast till noon. ⓐ 47–48 Thomas Hand St ⓣ 01 849 2322 ⓛ 09.00–17.30 Mon–Sat, 10.00–17.30 Sun

AFTER DARK

Restaurants
Howth
Abbey Tavern ££ An 800-year-old tavern serving sound grub. Live music and Irish dancing after dinner in the evening. ⓐ Abbey St ⓣ 01 839 0307 ⓦ www.abbeytavern.ie ⓛ 10.30–23.30 (00.30 at weekends), lunch 12.30–15.00, dinner 19.30–21.30, show nightly in summer 20.45–22.30

El Paso ££ Big Tex-Mex place with covered outdoor seating area and lots of spicy Mexican favourites. ⓐ 10 Harbour Rd ⓣ 01 832 3334 ⓛ 18.30–23.00

Aqua ££–£££ Former exclusive yacht club now open to anyone with some plastic to flash. Lovely location with views over the harbour.

OUT OF TOWN

Fresh seafood and some meat dishes. Excellent value early-bird menu from 17.30. ⓐ 1 West Pier ⓣ 01 832 0690 ⓛ 13.00–16.00 & 17.30–02.30 Tues–Sun

King Sitric £££ Long-established seafood restaurant with good sea views. Some very fresh and esoteric fish fill the menu. ⓐ East Pier ⓣ 01 832 5235 ⓛ 12.00–15.00 & 19.30–22.30 Mon–Sat

Malahide
Jaipur ££ Part of a successful chain of good Indian restaurants with classic Indian dishes, serving dinner from 17.30 to 23.00 daily. ⓐ St James Terrace ⓣ 01 845 5455

The Mad Fish ££ Stylish modern setting for respectable modern cooking. ⓐ White Sands Hotel, Portmarnock ⓣ 01 846 0420 ⓛ 18.30–21.30 Tues–Sat

Skerries
Stoop Your Head £–££ Seaside restaurant doing some good seafood. ⓐ Harbour Rd ⓣ 01 849 2085 ⓛ 12.00–14.30 & 18.00–21.30

Red Bank ££–£££ Excellent seafood restaurant. Choose your food while snacking on lovely hors d'oeuvres and an aperitif. Great service in a fun atmosphere. No place for a romantic dinner for two but you'll get great food. ⓐ 7 Church St ⓣ 01 849 1005

Bars & Pubs
Malahide
Duffy's You can catch some traditional music on Thursday nights after 21.00. ⓐ Main St ⓣ 01 845 0735

THE NORTHERN COASTLINE & NEWGRANGE

Gibney's With live music and a comedy club. ⓐ New St ⓣ 01 845 0863

Smyth's Lounge Live music. ⓐ New St ⓣ 01 845 0960

▲ Choose a fish supper from a local vendor

OUT OF TOWN

Skerries
The village has several places where you can catch some (mostly traditional) live music in the evenings. Pubs generally put up notices outside telling you what's on offer each week. A couple of good spots are:

Joe May's Has live music sessions on Friday nights. ⓐ Harbour Rd ⓣ 01 849 1241

Nealon's Has music mid-week, usually on Thursdays. ⓐ 12 Church St ⓣ 01 849 0061

ACCOMMODATION

Howth
Marine Hotel £–££ A little out of the way of Howth village but with lots of facilities that make up for it, and it's just a hop away from the Sutton Cross DART station. Pool, sauna, carvery lunch, good hotel dinner. ⓐ Sutton Cross ⓣ 01 839 0000 ⓦ www.marinehotel.ie

King Sitric ££ Small guesthouse and restaurant with an excellent reputation. All eight rooms have sea views. In the heart of Howth village. ⓐ East Pier ⓣ 01 832 5235 ⓦ www.kingsitric.ie

Malahide
White Sands Hotel ££ A bit inaccessible for the city, but this place has an amazing location with sweeping sea views and a well-run, cosy atmosphere. Live music in the bar. Very useful place if you are

THE NORTHERN COASTLINE & NEWGRANGE

driving, or there is a bus into Malahide right outside the hotel. Good value for what you get. ⓐ Coast Rd, Portmarnock ⓣ 01 866 6000 ⓦ www.whitesandshotel.ie

Skerries
Redbank House ££ Seriously worth considering as a place to stay, Skerries has the added advantage of this excellent guesthouse where breakfast is the highlight of the day. Lots of golfers use this as a base. ⓐ 5–7 Church St ⓣ 01 849 1005

▲ *Nealon's – traditional pub by day, club by night*

OUT OF TOWN

South of the city

Like its northern counterpart, the south of the city has formed from a series of small, quiet villages into an urban string. House prices rise as you leave the city, and the sea views, access to marinas and rural atmosphere explain why. Wandering around the streets and bars of Dalkey or Killiney you may well stumble upon the occasional Irish celeb, many of whom have settled in the area. Despite the urban sprawl, there is still much to see, most of it dominated by the overpowering and often grey outlines of Dublin Bay. As with the northern route, the familiar and clunky DART will take you to your destination, offering unreal seascapes out of a commuter transport system window. Again, sights are listed according to the order in which you will approach them by the train travelling south.

SIGHTS & ATTRACTIONS

Booterstown When the train stops at Booterstown, from your DART window (or if you have a mind, jump off the train and look) you can see a tiny wildlife sanctuary right beside the station. The little marsh here is home to some interesting sea and marsh bird life, which doesn't seem at all put off by the great green trains lumbering past every 20 minutes or so.

Dun Laoghaire

Rapidly becoming an urban centre in its own right Dun Laoghaire was, before the advent of budget airlines, the first place that visitors to Ireland encountered and, for those who bring their car over, it still is. With the ferry terminal close by and transport into the city so easy, this would make a good base for a stay in Dublin, particularly if

OUT OF TOWN

the 24-hour life of the city begins to pall. Its grand Victorian houses and seafront are reminders of the time when it was a major holiday destination for Dubliners and its newer malls and café bars reflect the consumer lifestyle of its present-day inhabitants. The **Dun Laoghaire Piers**, two piers which protect Dun Laoghaire harbour, are each over a mile long and both make a pleasant, if breezy, walk with views from the ends over Dublin Bay.

National Maritime Museum
One of those clunky little museums put together by enthusiasts, containing a longboat captured from the French invaders of 1798, a large lens from the Bailey lighthouse at Howth and lots of model ships. It is set in the former Mariners' Church.

ⓐ Haigh Terrace, Dun Laoghaire ⓣ 01 280 0969 ⓒ 13.00–17.00 (Apr–end Sep); admission charge ⓝ DART: Dun Laoghaire

Forty Foot
Named after the regiment which was once stationed here, the Forty Foot is a bathing place traditionally used only by men who wore no bathing clothes. You can still see the occasional nudist but now it is a mixed bathing area.

ⓐ Sandycove Point ⓝ Bus: 59 from Dun Laoghaire; DART: Sandycove

James Joyce Museum
James Joyce lived in this Martello tower for a week with his friend Oliver St John Gogarty and made it the scene of one of the opening pages of his novel *Ulysses*. Joyce fans will be able to re-create the scene and admire Joyce's guitar, some of his letters, and some rare first editions of his work. The tower is set out as it would have been when St John Gogarty lived there and you can go up to the roof for the views.

SOUTH OF THE CITY

○ Joyce Tower, Sandycove Point ○ 01 280 9265
○ www.dublintourism.com ○ 10.00–13.00 & 14.00–17.00 Mon–Sat, 14.00–18.00 Sun & public holidays (Mar–Oct); admission charge
○ Bus: 59 from Dun Laoghaire; DART: Sandycove

Dalkey

Dublin's answer to Beverly Hills, Dalkey teems with ageing rock stars, celebrity chefs and actors waiting for that call to collect their Oscar. Besides the pretty coastal walks here, the main attraction is **Dalkey Castle**, one of six towers that once stood in the area and which were used to store goods brought into what was once Dublin's major harbour. Inside you can see the murder hole which defenders used to drop heavy objects down onto people they didn't like the look of, and other medieval features. The tower also serves as a heritage centre and guided walks of the area leave from here.
○ Castle St, Dalkey ○ 01 285 8366 ○ www.dalkeycastle.com
○ 09.30–17.00 Mon–Fri, historical walks 11.45 Mon, 13.45 Wed, 11.45 Fri ○ DART: Dalkey

Bray

Bray is a quiet, almost sleepy little Victorian seaside town which is filled with B&Bs and has a Victorian seafront complete with shingle beach. It is perfect for a day when the city just becomes too much and you need some space. The highlight of a trip to Bray is the 8-km (5-mile) cliff walk from **Bray to Greystones**. It is a bracing walk along clearly marked footpaths and the start can be found at the southern end of the promenade. From the village of Greystones it is possible to catch bus 84 back to Bray. A shorter but more strenuous walk can be undertaken to the top of **Bray Head** from the same starting point. The path climbs to the top of the hill, offering stunning views

OUT OF TOWN

over the Wicklow Mountains and all the way to Wales on a clear day. A less energetic option is a visit to the **National Sea Life Centre**, where you'll find 70 species of sea-living creatures, both local and otherwise, including shark, piranha, armour-plated starlet and more. Feeding times, talks and presentations are all on offer.

National Sea Life Centre ⓐ Strand Road, Bray, Wicklow ⓣ 01 286 6939 ⓦ www.sealife.ie ⓛ 10.00–18.00 (May–Sept); 11.00–17.00 (Oct–Apr); last admission one hour before closing; admission charge ⓝ DART: Bray

Enniskerry

Although it is only 19 km (12 miles) out of Dublin, you are definitely out of the city when you visit this bustling little market town at the foot of the Wicklow Hills. The town owes its existence to the Wingfield family who laid out the original village in the 18th century. There are several interesting cafés which make this a good starting or finishing point for a walk in the hills, but the chief reason to visit is to see **Powerscourt Gardens**. The huge Powerscourt estate was created by the same Richard Wingfield who built the first rows of workers' cottages for his employees. At the heart of it is Powerscourt House, built by Richard Castle in the first half of the 18th century. Sadly, the house was gutted by fire in 1974, just after it had been fully renovated, and restoration had to begin again and continues still. The real reason why hundreds of people make the

> **SPIRIT-FILLED INSPIRATION**
> The story goes that the 19th-century designer of the Powerscourt Gardens, Daniel Robinson, was wheeled round the gardens in a wheelbarrow while he drank sherry to encourage his design skills to get to work.

SOUTH OF THE CITY

visit here is to see the gardens, 20 hectares (49 acres) of parkland and formal gardens. The gardens were first laid out in the 18th century and then altered in the 19th. On entering the gardens you are given a map which highlights several different hour-long walks around the gardens, pointing out unusual and specimen plants. The sights include a Japanese garden, Italian garden, a pet cemetery, fountains and other statuary. A signposted walk of 6 km (4 miles)

▲ *Powerscourt Gardens – imagine living here*

OUT OF TOWN

takes you to Powerscourt Waterfall, a 130-m (426-ft) fall of water, the highest in the British Isles and well worth the trek.

ⓐ Powerscourt Estate, Enniskerry ⓣ 01 204 6000
ⓦ www.powerscourt.ie ⓛ house and gardens 09.30–17.30 (shorter hours in winter), waterfall 09.30–19.00 (summer); 10.30–dusk (winter); admission charge ⓝ Bus: 44 from Hawkins St, Dublin

Russborough House

This is probably the finest extant house built in the Palladian style, with a great long string of curlicues and bits and pieces extending the front aspect of the house into an ornate wall far bigger than the house itself. It, like lots of the other houses in this style, was built in the mid-18th century, before the Act of Union put paid to the economic upsurgence of Ireland. Richard Castle built it for Joseph Leeson, or Lord Russborough, who, like many of his wealthy contemporaries, made his money from alcohol. In the 1950s the house passed into the hands of the people who owned the De Beers Diamond mines and who brought to the house their art collection, most of which was later donated to the National Gallery. One of the chief reasons for coming here is to see the paintings from the collection which are displayed here – the exhibits change regularly. Visit is by tour, which takes in the important paintings. A second tour visits the bedrooms with their displays of silverware and furniture.

ⓐ 5 km (3 miles) south west of Blessington ⓣ 045 865 239
ⓛ 10.30–17.30 (1 May–Sept); Sun & public holidays only (Oct–end Apr); admission charge ⓝ Bus: 65 from Eden Quay (90 minutes)

ⓞ *The distinctive 'round tower' at Glendalough*

OUT OF TOWN

The Wicklow Way
Wicklow is considered the garden of Dublin and some beautiful walks are possible through unspoiled countryside. The easiest way to experience hill-walking in the Wicklow Hills is to follow part of the Wicklow Way, a signposted walking route of 211 km (131 miles). Although it is signposted it is important to carry a map of the route and a compass, as it's easy to get lost on the many crossing paths. East-West Mapping (see page 155) produces a strip map, and OS Discovery series maps 50, 56 and 62 cover the whole of the route.

Glendalough
This is a series of medieval monastic sites set in some of Wicklow's most picturesque countryside. A trip here can involve little more than an hour-long guided tour around the sites or it can extend to a day's walk around the lakes or around Spink mountain using one of the guided walk books available from Easons (see page 95) or other bookshops. Set beside the R756, the **Glendalough Visitor Centre** offers an introduction to the two monastic sites, a small museum containing some of the stonework and a short audio-visual presentation on their history. The centre has leaflets describing what you will see and outlining one or two short walks around the lake. It is not necessary to pay the entrance fee to the visitor centre to go on to the lake or the ruins.

Two minutes away from the visitor centre is the first of the sites, the **Lower Lake Monastic Sites**, with the 10th-century round tower dominating the landscape and the ruins of the cathedral. The 12th-century priest's house was heavily restored in the 19th century. The most beautiful and intact building is St Kevin's Church, a two-storey oratory with a belfry. Also here is St Saviour's, a 12th-century Romanesque church with much of its decoration intact.

SOUTH OF THE CITY

> **THE WAY TO SEE THE COUNTRY**
> Here's what awaits you if you decide to take on the Wicklow Way – well, the first two days anyway:
> Day 1: Join the route at Marlay Park in the south of Dublin (Bus: 47B). The walk travels south for 21 km (13 miles), is well signposted and well used by other walkers. The route passes through Kilmashogue Lane , through woods of the same name and up Two Rock Mountain to Glencullen, then across open moorland to Knockree, where there is a hostel, or you can make your way to Enniskerry (no bus service).
> Day 2: The finest walk of all takes you past the Powerscourt Waterfall and then into the Wicklow Hills with Sugarloaf and Maulin mountains as a backdrop. The route follows the Dargle River for a time and then reaches Lough Tay and carries on to Glendalough; a stiff walk of 29 km (18 miles). You can recuperate with hearty fare and a comfy bed at Glendalough.

If all this medieval ruin hasn't been enough, you can walk on to the second set of ruins, the **Upper Lake Monastic Sites**. Here is Reefert Church, another Romanesque-style building, while a little further along is St Kevin's cell, a beehive hut, so called because it is built from corbelled slates, each one sitting a little above the other, forming a beehive shape. Monks would have come here to be alone and meditate. A path leads to a small waterfall and further on is St Kevin's Bed, a cave where the monk who founded this place is said to have spent some time.

Visitor Centre ❶ 0404 45425 ❷ 09.30–17.15 (mid-Mar–Oct); 09.30–16.15 (Nov–mid-Mar); admission charge and charge for leaflets on history and walks ❸ Bus: St Kevin's Bus (❶ 01 281 8119 ❹ www.

OUT OF TOWN

glendaloughbus.com) departs daily from opposite the Mansion House in Dawson St, Dublin, at 11.30 & 18.00 Mon–Sat, 11.30 & 19.00 Sun, return services are 07.15 & 16.15 Mon–Fri, 09.45 & 17.40 Sat & Sun

RETAIL THERAPY

Avoca Handweavers Huge branch of the craft emporium set in a little sight of its own, a 19th-century garden with some rare specimens of trees and plants. Rare, too, is the inexpensive café serving good food (see below). ⓐ Kilmacnogue, 4 km (2½ miles) south of Bray on N11 ⓣ 01 286 7466 ⓒ 09.00–18.00 Mon–Fri, 09.30–18.00 Sat, Sun & bank holidays ⓝ Bus: 145 from Mountjoy Square, Dublin, or pick it up at Bray DART station

Blackrock Market Full of interesting clothes, bric-a-brac, antiques and handicrafts. ⓐ Blackrock, three stops before Dun Laoghaire on the DART ⓒ Sun

TAKING A BREAK

Dun Laoghaire
Mao Café Bar ££ Branch of the city centre cafeteria. No-nonsense, cafeteria-style Asian fusion with Malay, Thai, Chinese, Turkish and other influences. Seating outside. ⓐ Pavilion Centre ⓣ 01 214 8090 ⓒ 12.00–22.30 Mon–Thur, 12.00–23.00 Fri & Sat, 12.00–22.00 Sun

Bray
Avoca Handweavers £ Self-service restaurant with some excellent and original food. If you like it, buy the cookbook. ⓐ Kilmacnogue ⓣ 01 286 7466 ⓒ 09.30–17.00 Mon–Fri, 10.00–17.00 Sat & Sun

SOUTH OF THE CITY

Enniskerry

Powerscourt Terrace Café £ In the remains of Powerscourt House, this self-service place is another branch of Avoca and is worth seeking out. You don't have to pay the entrance fee for the gardens to find the café. ☎ 01 204 6070 or 01 204 6000 ⏰ 09.30–17.30

Powerscourt Arms Hotel £–££ Bar food and restaurant serving respectable hotel grub. 📍 Main St ☎ 01 282 8903 ⏰ 12.30–14.30 & 18.00–21.00 Mon-Fri, 12.30–21.00 Sat & Sun

◔ *Take a seat at the Purple Ocean Restaurant*

OUT OF TOWN

AFTER DARK

Restaurants
Dun Laoghaire
The Queen's ££ A pub/restaurant complex with big-screen tellies and upstairs piano bar/restaurant. ⓐ 12 Castle St, Dalkey ⓣ 01 285 4569

Purple Ocean Restaurant £££ Modern Irish seafood, harbour views and outdoor seating. ⓐ St Michael's Pier, Dun Laoghaire ⓣ 01 284 5590 ⓦ www.purpleocean.ie ⓛ 19.30–23.00

Roly@The Pavilion £££ This is a branch of the Roly's in Ballsbridge. Modern Irish cuisine in luxurious surroundings. The set dinner menu brings this place down in price to ££. ⓐ Pavilion Centre ⓣ 01 236 0286 ⓛ 12.00–22.00 Tues–Sat, 12.00–20.00 Sun

ACCOMMODATION

Avondale House £ Small and very basic B&B in a Victorian house. ⓐ 3 Northumberland Ave, Dun Laoghaire ⓣ 01 280 9628

Rochestown Lodge Hotel and Leisure Club ££ Recently revamped. Facilities include pool, fitness centre, sauna. ⓐ Rochestown Ave, Dun Laoghaire ⓣ 01 285 3555 ⓦ www.rochestownlodge.com

◑ *Mural of the Táin Bó Cuailgne by Kilkenny centre*

PRACTICAL information

PRACTICAL INFORMATION

Directory

GETTING THERE
By air
From UK: Dublin airport has connections with 28 British airports and most airlines make their prices as competitive as they can, offering a few cheap seats on each flight and very cheap rates at off-peak times, and charging the earth at peak times. Book as far in advance as you can and try to travel off-peak. It can occasionally be cheaper to book two single flights rather than a return. Flight time from most British cities is about one hour.

Airlines operating from UK:
Aer Arann ❶ 0800 5872324 Ⓦ www.aerarann.com
Aer Lingus ❶ 0845 084444 Ⓦ www.aerlingus.com
Air Wales ❶ 0870 7773131 Ⓦ www.airwales.co.uk
bmibaby ❶ 0870 2642229 Ⓦ www.bmibaby.com
British Airways ❶ 0870 8509850 Ⓦ www.britishairways.com
easyJet ❶ 0870 6000000 Ⓦ www.easyjet.com
Flybe ❶ 08705 676676 Ⓦ www.flybe.com
Flybmi ❶ 0870 6070555 Ⓦ www.flybmi.com
Ryanair ❶ 0871 2460000 Ⓦ www.ryanair.com

From Europe: There are numerous connections between Dublin and most European countries with Ryanair, Aer Lingus, bmibaby and flybmi offering budget flights.
From North America: There are direct flights from seven US eastern cities to Dublin, mostly via Shannon. Flights from other cities cost considerably more and it often works out cheaper to fly to London Heathrow, Gatwick or Stansted and make a connection to one of the

DIRECTORY

budget airlines. From Canada, Air Canada flies to Dublin via Heathrow from Montreal, Vancouver and Toronto. Again, check the price of a flight to London and a separate ticket from there to Ireland. Check out Aer Lingus, Delta Airlines, Royal Jordanian, Continental Airlines and Air Canada.

From Australia and New Zealand: There are no direct flights to Dublin and you are best to check out flights to London and on to Dublin independently rather than use companies offering connections. Check the websites of Aer Lingus, Air New Zealand, British Airways, KLM, Malaysia Airlines, Qantas and Singapore Airlines.

Many people are aware that air travel emits CO_2, which contributes to climate change. You may be interested in the possibility of lessening the environmental impact of your flight through the charity Climate Care, which offsets your CO_2 by funding environmental projects around the world. Visit www.climatecare.org

By sea

There are two entry points into the city by ferry: Dun Laoghaire and Dublin Port in the city.

Irish Ferries Sail from Holyhead to Dublin Port (3¼ hours). ☏ 08705 171717 ⓦ www.irishferries.ie

Sea Cat Sail from Liverpool (4 hours) and the Isle of Man (2¾ hours). ☏ 08705 523523 ⓦ www.seacat.co.uk

Stena Line Sail from Holyhead to Dun Laoghaire (1½ hours) and to Dublin Port (3½ hours). ☏ 08705 707070 ⓦ www.stenaline.com

By road

Several coach companies operate a Dublin-London trip. This can be the cheapest means of transport but is certainly the slowest.

National Express Eurolines Runs regular daily services from London

PRACTICAL INFORMATION

to Dublin via Birmingham (12 hours). ❶ 08705 143219
Ⓦ www.eurolines.co.uk
Slattery's Has daily services from London, Bristol, Birmingham, Reading, Liverpool, Manchester and Leeds. ❶ 0800 515900
Ⓦ www.slatterys.com

By rail

Ireland has a complex network of rail routes operated by Iarnród Éireann (www.irishrail.ie) connecting with Connolly Station or Heuston Station in Dublin. Belfast trains connect with Connolly Station, while trains from cities in the south of Ireland connect with Heuston. Stena Line offers a train/ferry package from London to Dublin.

ENTRY FORMALITIES

All visitors to Dublin from abroad need a valid passport except British nationals who do, however, need some form of photographic ID. EU citizens may stay in Dublin indefinitely without a visa. Visitors from the USA, Canada, Australia and New Zealand may stay for three months without a visa and this can be extended at Harcourt St Garda Síochána (Police Station).

CUSTOMS

For EU travellers there are no customs duties and no duty free restrictions, although you may have to show that the items you bring in are for personal use and not for resale. Travellers from outside the EU can bring in 200 cigarettes, 1 litre of spirits or 2 litres of wine, 60 ml of perfume and 250 ml of toilet water. Pets can travel from Britain and Northern Ireland without quarantine. Dogs and cats from the EU may be brought into the country if they have been

DIRECTORY

fitted with a microchip, vaccinated against rabies and blood-tested six months before entry.

MONEY

Ireland is a member of the Eurozone. This has seven banknotes – €5, €10, €20, €50, €100, €200 and €500. Coins come in denominations of €1, €2 and 1, 2, 5, 10, 20 and 50 cents. 24-hour ATMs are located outside most banks, in railway stations and at the airport, and will accept cards with Cirrus and Maestro symbols. You can also withdraw cash using Visa, Access and MasterCard. Visa and MasterCard are universally accepted, although you will need a PIN. American Express and Diners' Club cards are less widely used.

Travellers' cheques are a safe way of carrying money and can be changed at post offices and banks, although a commission will be

● *A convenient tram service runs through the city*

PRACTICAL INFORMATION

charged. You will need some form of photographic identification. Changing cash can be an expensive business, especially in hotels. The best rates are at the banks but there are also bureaux de change, which operate outside banking hours. Visitors from outside the EU can obtain a refund of VAT on purchases if they leave within two months and if the shop their item was purchased from belongs to the Retail Export Scheme.

HEALTH, SAFETY & CRIME
Health
No special health precautions are necessary before arriving in Ireland. Tap water is safe to drink. EU citizens are entitled to the same medical care as Irish citizens although you must bring a European Health Insurance Card (EHIC) with you. The British website for ordering these cards is www.ehic.org.uk. (This replaces the old E111 form.) A visit to a GP in Ireland will entail a consultation fee, although any tests will be included in the price. A prescription charge will be levied for any medicines, around €15 for each item. These fees are not refundable. In Dublin a consultation will cost around €40. Visitors from both the UK and outside Europe should seriously consider medical insurance when visiting Ireland, although emergency medical treatment is free. Contraception is available over the counter in Ireland but the 'morning after' pill can be obtained only on prescription. In an emergency at weekends the Family Planning Association, 5/7 Cathal Brugha St ❶ 01 872 7088 is open 09.00-16.00 Sat, 14.00-17.00 Sun. ❶ All public buildings are smoke-free areas.

Safety & crime
Like all big cities, Dublin has its share of street crime. Personal belongings should be taken care of and kept out of sight. Carry a

DIRECTORY

shoulder bag across the chest rather than hanging from a shoulder. Take care at ATMs in particular. Car break-ins are also commonplace. While it is safe to walk around most of the well-lit and busy city centre streets until late into the evening, things can get quite rowdy in the early hours at weekends in Temple Bar, O'Connell Street, Camden Street, Grafton Street and Harcourt Street. Needless to say, Phoenix Park is not a safe place at night. Dublin also has its share of beggars who, for the most part, are model citizens compared with the drunken hen parties at 02.00. Many sell the *Big Issue* magazine and carry certification.

Hitchhiking was once common in Ireland, even in Dublin. It is still fairly safe in rural areas but is not recommended around Dublin, particularly if you are alone. Another hazard in Dublin is traffic. If it isn't gridlocked, it is travelling very quickly through the city streets and crossing roads can be hazardous. College Green, the junction in front of Trinity College, is particularly hazardous since speeding traffic travels from several different directions as the lights change and pedestrians get tired of waiting to cross safely. In other places there simply is no way to cross safely, and in others you can set off to cross when the green man flashes and halfway across the junction he's turned red.

The police force is called Garda Síochána; officers wear navy blue uniforms and travel in blue and white cars labelled Garda Síochána. Usually spoken of as guards, they generally do not carry guns. Pairs of pedestrian guards are an occasional sight around the main shopping streets and in Temple Bar. They become much more visible in the early hours, especially at weekends.

❶ Possession of even tiny amounts of cannabis is a crime in Ireland and will not be ignored.

PRACTICAL INFORMATION

> **HEALTH INFORMATION**
> British government health and travel advice:
> www.doh.gov.uk/travellers & www.fco.gov.uk/travel
> American sites for travellers: www.cdc.gov/travel &
> www.healthfinder.com
> World Health Organization: www.who.int/en
> Travel Health Online: www.travelhealth.co.uk
> Basic travel information on different countries:
> www.brookes.ac.uk/worldwise
> Useful tips and information: www.tripprep.com

OPENING HOURS

Shops are generally open 09.00–17.30 Mon–Sat, with many of the city centre stores opening later and staying open until 20.00 on Thursdays, and open 13.00–17.00 on Sundays. Banking hours are usually 10.00–16.00 Mon–Fri. Some banks open late on Thursdays.

TOILETS

There are public toilets in all shopping centres and department stores, and toilets for customers' use in restaurants and bars. There is usually a small charge to use those in shopping centres and bartenders can occasionally get shirty if you just wander in and use the toilet. Toilets are marked by little men and women symbols on the doors but might occasionally be marked *fir* for men or *mná* for women.

CHILDREN

Dublin loves children and is a child-friendly city, apart from the traffic. Children are welcome in pubs during the day and restaurants

DIRECTORY

often have child seats and menus or will serve half portions. There are lots of green spaces playing in and amusing statuary all over the city to climb over. Even travelling on the DART is fun. Sights that are particularly suited to children include:

- **Bray** (see page 133) The National Sea Life Centre, with petting zoo, train rides, a beach and a hill to climb.

- **Dublinia** (see page 77) There are smells, things to poke and people dressed up in silly costumes.

- **Dublin Zoo** (see page 100) Petting zoo, train rides, animal shows…

- **Fry Model Railway & Tara's Palace** Although it's a 'look but don't touch' kind of place, it's still a fascinating way to spend a few hours.

- **Liffey Voyage** A river trip which departs from a landing station off the boardwalk at Bachelors Walk. ⓐ Bachelors Walk ⓘ 01 473 4082 ⓦ www.liffeyvoyage.ie

- **St Michan's Church** (see page 108) Not for the squeamish, most kids will be morbidly fascinated by the mummified bodies.

- **Viking Splash Tour** Possibly the silliest activity in the city, this is an amphibious vehicle, decorated to look like a longboat, which tours the Viking sites of the city and then drives into the Grand Canal Harbour. The pick-up point is beside St Patrick's Cathedral or St Stephen's Green. ⓘ 01 707 6000 ⓦ www.vikingsplashtours.com ⓞ tours depart 10.30, 12.00 & 14.00, and last 1¼ hours; admission charge

PRACTICAL INFORMATION

COMMUNICATIONS
Telephones
Public phones in Ireland take both credit cards and coins. You can also buy pre-paid phone cards from newsagents and 24-hour grocery stores. Avoid using the phone in your hotel bedroom; hotel rates can be very high.

Mobile phones
Your mobile phone should work in Ireland if you have instructed your provider to turn on the 'roaming' option. Before you use it, check how much it will cost to use. Companies often charge for receiving texts and phone calls as well as making calls from abroad.

Post
The main GPO is in O'Connell Street. There are sub-post offices in Parnell Street, Aston Place, Earlsfort Terrace, Merrion Row, Parkgate Street, Usher's Quay, Ormond Quay Upper and Andrew Street (🕓 09.00–17.30 Mon–Fri, 09.00–13.00 Sat). A 50 g letter to a destination in Ireland or Northern Ireland is €0.48 and the same letter to Britain or the rest of the world costs €0.75. See www.anpost.ie
O'Connell Street GPO 📞 01 705 7000 🕓 08.00–20.00 Mon–Sat, 10.00–18.30 Sun & bank holidays

Internet
Most hotels and hostels have internet access for guests and there are internet cafés located around the city. Try:
Global Internet Café @ 8 Lower O'Connell St 📞 01 878 0295

ELECTRICITY

The electricity supply is 220–240 volts, 50 Hertz. Plugs have 3 square pins as in the UK. Adapters for US and European appliances can be bought at the airport, from electrical shops around the city or from Dublin Tourism (see page 154).

TELEPHONING DUBLIN

Dublin phone numbers have 7 digits. If you are calling from outside the city you must add the area code (01). To call from abroad, dial the international code first (usually 00), then the country code (353), the area code minus the initial 0, and the local number.

TELEPHONING FROM DUBLIN

When phoning other areas in Ireland from Dublin, you must first dial the area code, then the phone number. To phone abroad, dial 00 first, then the country code, followed by the area code (minus the initial 0 if there is one) and the local number.

Country codes:

Australia 61
Canada 1
France 33
Germany 49
New Zealand 64
South Africa 27
UK 44
USA 1

National directory (Ireland and Northern Ireland) 11811 or 11818
International directory (including UK) 11850 or 11860

PRACTICAL INFORMATION

DISABLED TRAVELLERS

All newer buildings and public transport have wheelchair access and most hotels have disabled-friendly rooms. For individual bus routes contact Dublin Bus. DART and Iarnród Éireann are less disabled-friendly simply because they are older, although ramps can be provided with prior notice. Restaurants must provide disabled toilet facilities. Some of the city's sights may be inaccessible to wheelchair users. For more information, contact the following:

Dublin Bus Customer Service 59 O'Connell St 01 873 4222 www.dublinbus.ie

Iarnród Éireann Offers the free booklet *Guide for Mobility-impaired Passengers.* 01 703 2369

Irish Wheelchair Association 01 818 6400 www.iwa.ie

National Disability Authority 01 608 0400 www.nda.ie

Restaurants Association of Ireland Provides the free booklet *Dining in Ireland.* 01 677 9901

FURTHER INFORMATION

Tourist offices

Dublin Tourism is a walk-in service (no telephone) and includes accommodation advice and bookings, ferry, sport and concert tickets, a car hire desk, free leaflets and an extensive book and map shop. St Andrew's Church, Suffolk St

Other offices around the city are at the following:

Arrivals Hall Dublin Airport Accommodation advice and booking, ferry, sport and concert tickets and general information. 08.00–22.00

14 O'Connell St Upper Less crowded and friendlier than the hyper-busy Suffolk St branch, and useful for general information and booking accommodation. 09.00–17.00

Dun Laoghaire Ferry Terminal 🕐 10.00–18.00 Mon–Sat
Fáilte Ireland @ Baggot St Bridge 🕐 09.30–12.00 & 12.30–17.00
Temple Bar Information Centre For information about what's on in Temple Bar. @ 12 East Essex St ⓦ www.visit-templebar.com

Tourist websites
General www.tourismireland.com
Australia www.tourismireland.com.au
France www.irland-tourisme.fr
Germany www.irishtouristboard.de
USA www.shamrock.org

FURTHER READING
At Swim, Two Boys by J O'Neill (Scribner). Love and politics in Dublin.
Dublin by Joss Lynam (Gill & Macmillan). 35 walks in the Dublin region.
Dublin: A Celebration by Pat Liddy (Dublin Corporation). Too big for your suitcase but check it out in the national library for the low-down on all the major buildings and statuary.
The Complete Wicklow Way by J B Malone (O'Brien Press). A guide to the long-distance walk.
The Irish Heritage Cookbook by Margaret Johnson (Wolfhound Press). Try out some of the dishes you've enjoyed in Dublin.
The Rising by B Tóibin (New Island Books). Love story set in the days leading up to the Easter Rising 1916.
The Speckled People by Hugo Hamilton (Fourth Estate). Biographical account of a boy growing up in Dublin.
The Truth about the Irish by Terry Eagleton (New Island Books). Everything you wanted to know but were afraid to ask.
The Wicklow Way (East-West Mapping Ballyredmond, Enniscorthy, County Wexford ☎ 054 77835).

PRACTICAL INFORMATION

Emergencies

MEDICAL EMERGENCIES

In a medical emergency call 999 for an ambulance. If your condition is not so serious, you can contact the Eastern Region Health Authority (❶ 01 620 1600), which has a list of doctors. Your hotel will also be able to supply a contact for a GP. Out of surgery hours there is a private organisation called Doctors on Call, who will come to where you are, for a fee. Alternatively, you can go to one of the A&E departments of the city's hospitals:

Mater Misericordiae Hospital Closest to the city centre. ⓐ Eccles St ❶ 01 830 2000 ❷ 24 hours

St Vincent's ⓐ Merrion Rd ❶ 01 269 4533

In a dental emergency during working hours, go to the Dental Hospital. Between 17.00 and 23.00, phone the hospital and you will be contacted within 2 hours by a dentist. After 23.00 you must go to a regular A&E (see above).

Dublin Dental Hospital ⓐ Lincoln Place ❶ 01 612 7200
❷ 09.00–17.00

POLICE

There are police stations (identified by a blue lamp above the door with 'Garda' written on it) in the following:

> **EMERGENCY NUMBERS**
> **Ambulance** 999
> **Fire** 999
> **Police** 999
> **Doctors** on call (after hours) 01 453 9333

EMERGENCIES

Store St 01 666 8000
Fitzgibbon St 01 666 8400
Pearse St 01 666 9000
Harcourt Square 01 666 6666

LOST OR STOLEN CARDS

You should make a note before you travel of the number to ring in the event of a lost or stolen credit card. Any theft should be reported to Tourism Victim Support (Garda HQ, Harcourt Square 01 478 5295). An incident report should be collected for insurance purposes.

EMBASSIES

Australia Fitzwilliam House, Wilton Terrace 01 664 5300, after-hours emergency freephone to Canberra 1800 556 197 office hours

New Zealand In an emergency contact the New Zealand embassy in London. 00 44 20 7930 8422 www.nzembassy.com/uk

South Africa Alexandra House, Earlsfort Centre, Earlsfort Terrace 01 660 4233, after-hours emergency phone 087 050 6934 office hours

UK For lost passports, you must wait till office hours or return to Britain without one (but get a police report). 31 Merrion Rd 01 205 3700, after-hours emergency (arrest, serious accident) phone 086 243 4655 office hours

USA 42 Elgin Rd 01 661 5553, after-hours emergency phone 01 668 9464

INDEX

A
accommodation 34–39, 128–129, 142
air travel 144–145
airport 48
Ardgillan Castle 122
arts *see* culture

B
Bank of Ireland 60
bars, clubs & pubs 25–26, 27, 28–30, 70, 71–73, 74, 83–85, 96, 98–99, 110–114, 124–125, 127–128
Bloomsday 12–13
Boardwalk 86
boat travel 52, 145, 151
The Book of Kells 60, 62, 64
Booterstown 130
Bray 133–134
Bray Head 133–134
bus travel 46, 48–49, 52, 53, 56, 116

C
cafés 46–47, 69, 96, 124–125
Chester Beatty Library 76
children 150–151
Chimney Tower 100
Christ Church Cathedral 76–77
cinema 30, 85
City Hall 74, 76
coach travel 52, 145–146
comedy 30, 84
crime 53, 104, 148–149, 157
culture 10, 18–20, 30, 45, 46, 64–65, 76–79, 85, 90–93, 104–110, 132–133, 136
Custom House Visitor Centre 88

customs & duty 146–147
cycling 58

D
Dalkey 133
Dalkey Castle 133
dance 19–20, 30
disabilities, travellers with 154
driving 53, 58
Dublin Castle 77
Dublin City Gallery: The Hugh Lane 91–92
Dublin Writer's Museum 92
Dublin Zoo 100, 103
Dublinia & Viking World 77
Dun Laoghaire 130, 132

E
electricity 153
embassies 157
emergencies 156–157
Enniskerry 134–136
entertainment 28–30 *see also* nightlife
events 8–13

F
ferry travel 52, 145
festivals 10, 11
food & drink 24–27, 68
Forty Foot 132
Four Courts 104
Francis Bacon studio 91
Fry Model Railway 119

G
Gaelic Football 32
Gallery of Photography 78
Garden of Remembrance 90
Glendalough 138–140
GPO building 88
Grafton Street 60, 66

Greystones 133
Guinness Storehouse 103

H
health 27, 148, 150, 156
history 14–15, 88, 89–90, 91, 104–106
hotels, guesthouses & hostels 34–39, 128–129, 142
Howth peninsula 116, 118
Howth village 116, 118

I
insurance 148
internet 152
Irish Jewish Museum 104–105
Irish Museum of Modern Art 105

J
The James Joyce Centre 92–93
James Joyce Museum 132–133
Joyce, James 12, 92, 132

K
Kildare Street 66
Kilmainham Gaol 105–106
Knowth 123

L
Lane, Hugh 91
lifestyle 16–17

M
Malahide Castle 46, 119
Malahide village 46, 118, 123
Marsh's Library 106
Meeting House Square 76
Merrion Square 62
money 53, 147–148, 157

INDEX

music 18–19, 28, 30, 72, 73, 83–85, 113–114, 127–128

N

National Gallery 64–65
National Maritime Museum 132
National Museum of Archaeology & History 65
National Museum of Decorative Arts & History at Collins Barracks 106, 108
National Museum of Natural History 65
National Photographic Archive 78–79
National Sea Life Centre 134
National Transport Museum 118
Newbridge House & Traditional Farm 120
Newgrange 116, 122–123
Newman House 62–63
nightlife 28–30, 70–73, 74, 81–85, 96, 98–99, 113–114, 125–128, 142
northern coastline 116

O

O'Connell Street 34, 86, 88–89, 93
Old Jameson Distillery 103
opening hours 11, 53–54, 150

P

Parnell Square 89–90
passports & visas 146, 157
Phoenix Park 104
phones 152, 153
police 149, 156–157

post 152
Powerscourt Gardens 134–135
Powerscourt House 134
Powerscourt Waterfall 135–136
Prospect Cemetery 108
public holidays 11
public transport 46, 48–49, 52–53, 56, 58, 116, 130, 146

R

rail travel 46, 52–53, 56, 58, 116, 130, 146
restaurants 24–25, 27, 69–71, 81–83, 95–96, 98, 113, 125–126, 141–142
Rotunda Maternity Hospital 90
Royal Hospital 105
Russborough House 136

S

safety 53, 104, 148–149
St Michan's Church 108–109
St Patrick's Cathedral 109–110
St Stephen's Green 25–27, 63
seasons 8
Shaw's Birthplace 110
Sheila na gigs 64
shopping 22–23, 66–68, 79–80, 93–95, 110, 123, 140, 148
Skerries Mills 121–122
Skerries village 120
south of the city 130
South Great George Street 28, 66
sport 10–11, 32–33
street art 18, 20

T

Tara's Palace 119–20
taxis 52, 58
Temple Bar 25, 28, 34, 74
theatre 18, 85
time differences 48
toilets 150
tourist information 154–155
tram travel 56, 58
Trinity College 63–64
29 Fitzwilliam Street Lower 63

U

Ulysses (Joyce) 12–13

V

Viking Splash Tour 151

W

weather 8, 46–47
west of city 100
Wicklow Way 138, 139
Wilde, Oscar 62
wildlife sanctuary 130

Y

Ye Olde Hurdy Gurdy Museum 118

Z

zoo 100, 103

ACKNOWLEDGEMENTS & FEEDBACK

The publishers would like to thank the following for supplying the copyright photographs for this book:
Aidan O'Rourke www.aidan.co.uk p93; Alamy Images pp19, 29, 83, 121, 129; Jurys Croke Park Hotel p37; Mark Zangig www.zanzig.com pp42, 59; Pictures Colour Library pp5, 17, 21, 24, 40–41, 49, 57, 107, 115, 135, 137; Robert Harding World Imagery pp7, 13, 45, 97, 111; Sherland Entertainments Ltd p71; TASCQ www.visit-templebar.com p9; all other pictures by Pat Levy

Copy editor: Anne McGregor
Proofreader: Lynn Bresler

Send your thoughts to
books@thomascook.com

- **Found a great bar, club, shop or must-see sight that we don't feature?**
- **Like to tip us off about any information that needs updating?**
- **Want to tell us what you love about this handy little guidebook and more importantly how we can make it even handier?**

Then here's your chance to tell all! Send us ideas, discoveries and recommendations today and then look out for your valuable input in the next edition of this title. As an extra 'thank you' from Thomas Cook Publishing, you'll be automatically entered into our exciting monthly prize draw.

Send an email to the above address (stating the book's title) or write to: CitySpots Project Editor, Thomas Cook Publishing, PO Box 227, The Thomas Cook Business Park, Unit 18, Coningsby Road, Peterborough PE3 8SB, UK.